CHOCOLATE

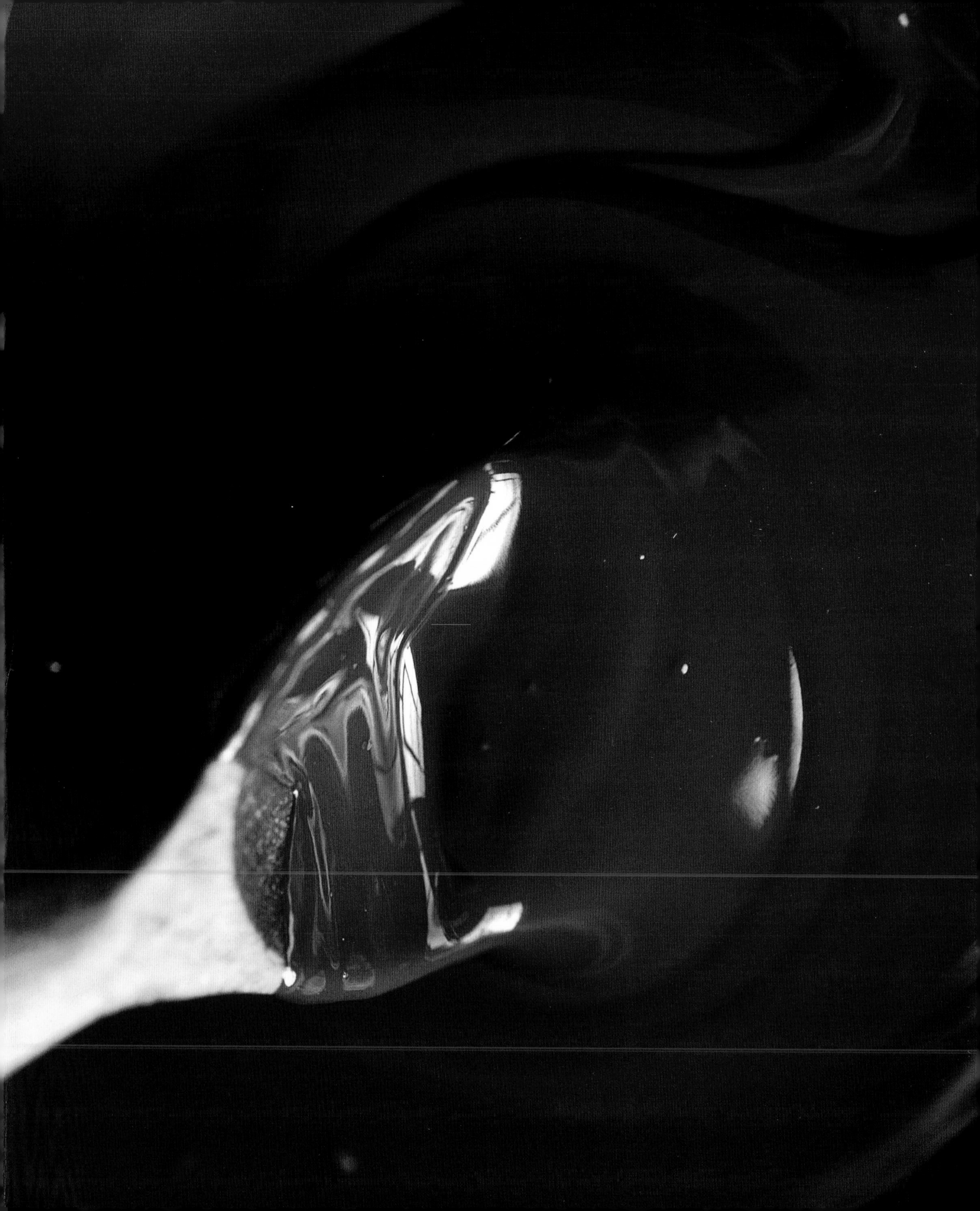

CHOCOLATE

deliciously indulgent recipes for chocolate lovers

Maxine Clark

photography by Peter Cassidy

RYLAND PETERS & SMALL

LONDON NEW YORK

Dedication

To Steve, a truly dedicated taster, tester, and gifted stylist

Design, photographic art direction, and prop styling Steve Painter
Editor Céline Hughes
Production Manager Patricia Harrington
Publishing Director Alison Starling

Food Stylist Maxine Clark
Assistant Food Stylists Joanna Lee, Jacks Clarke

Americanizer Susan Stuck
Indexer Diana Le Core

Notes

- All spoon measurements are level unless otherwise stated.
- Uncooked or partially cooked eggs should not be served to the very old, frail, young children, pregnant women or those with compromised immune systems.

Author's acknowledgments

Grateful thanks are due to the following people for help and advice:

Chloé Doutre-Roussel
The Chocolate Society
Martin Christy (www.seventypercent.com)
Pia Scavia, my Italian secret agent
Giacomo Biodi, Laboratorio Artigianale Giraudi (www.giraudi.it)
Lourdes Delgado, Ecuador
Graciela and Ian Mursell of Mexicolore, London
Dr. C.J. Turnbull, International Cocoa Germplasm Database, University of Reading
Dr Andrew Daymond, Cocoa Quarantine Project, University of Reading
Simon Harris of Barry Callebaut, UK

Ryland Peters & Small
Céline, my editor, for keeping me firmly on track
Alison Starling, for suggesting the book

The photographic team
Pete, you made it look so wonderful in both good and bad lights and a tight schedule
Steve, a designer with hidden styling talents—thanks for a beautiful, sensitive job
Jo, you are a joy to have in the kitchen!

First published in the United States in 2007
by Ryland Peters & Small, Inc.
519 Broadway, 5th Floor
New York, NY 10012
www.rylandpeters.com

10 9 8 7 6 5 4 3 2 1

ISBN-13: 978 1 84597 463 3
ISBN-10: 1 84597 463 8

Printed and bound in China

Library of Congress Cataloging-in-Publication Data
Clark, Maxine.
Chocolate : deliciously indulgent recipes for chocolate lovers / Maxine Clark ; photography by Peter Cassidy.
p. cm.
Includes index.
ISBN 978-1-84597-463-3
1. Cookery (Chocolate) 2. Chocolate desserts.
I. Title.
TX767.C5C57 2007
641.6'374--dc22

2007020345

CONTENTS

CHOCOLATE IS GOOD FOR YOU

If chocolate was considered the food of the gods by the ancient Aztec and Mayan civilizations, who are we to argue? We have always known that eating it makes us feel good (if a little guilty), but modern scientific research by The International Cocoa Organization (ICCO) has shown that the finely ground bean of the *Theobroma cacao* tree can be beneficial to health, and more than that—to personal well-being. In this sense, it's a bit of a wonder food.

We're not talking about chocolate in the form of sugary, mass-produced candy bars. Proper chocolate made with over 60% cocoa solids and few additives other than a little sugar and vanilla, when consumed in small doses, *is* good for you.

For chocoholics, eating chocolate is an incredible sensory experience: firstly, its rich and volatile aroma is released when the wrapping is reverently removed or the lid tentatively lifted from the box. Next comes the sight of its dark, mysterious, and lustrous form, then the sharp, satisfying snap as it breaks or is bitten. Finally, the longed-for moment when the chocolate is placed on the tongue and left to melt, gradually producing an explosion of hedonistic flavors (tropical fruit, licorice, tobacco, nuts) trapped within the crushed cacao bean and awaiting their release triggered by body heat.

This inimitable process is what gives chocolate its fabled aphrodisiac qualities, since there is in fact no proven scientific evidence for its aphrodisiac status. However, it *can* trigger the release of serotonin and endorphins, both of which contribute to that "feel-good factor." It also contains phenylethylamine, an amine known to effect aphrodisiac symptoms (and good for relieving hangovers!) A companion of the Spanish conquistador H. Cortès, who was offered cocoa on landing in Mexico in 1519, is recorded to have said: "...the pleasure of consuming chocolate keeps one traveling all day. It keeps exhaustion away, without one feeling the need to eat or to drink."

However, there *are* several scientific facts to show that chocolate is good for you. A 3½-oz bar of dark chocolate (60–70% cocoa solids—see page 15 for an explanation of cocoa solids) is packed with naturally occurring minerals, giving the following RDA (Recommended Daily Allowance): magnesium 33%, phosphorous 30%, potassium 27%, copper 25%, iron 20%, and calcium 13%. Dark chocolate is one of the foods richest in antioxidants, which have been shown to protect against the damaging effects of free radicals in the body. In fact, it is second only (I am reliably informed) to the prune—so you can imagine how good for you the Polish speciality of a prune dipped in dark chocolate is!

It's also good to know that cocoa butter contains "good" fats similar to those found in olive oil. A 3½-oz bar made from 72% cocoa solids contains 41 g fat—but 34 g of this is unsaturated fat, which raises good cholesterol (HDL), protects the heart, and lowers bad cholesterol (LDL). That leaves only 7 g saturated fat, the harmful effects of which are counterbalanced by the unsaturated fats. Thanks to modern scientific research, cacao flavonoids have been found to have a stronger antioxidant effect than those found in red wine or green tea. Cacao flavonoids can help to reduce the risk of heart attack (and possibly cancer), protect against arthritis, and even act as a natural antihistamine. Wow—we always knew chocolate was good for us, but we never imagined it was this good!

Theobromine, the alkaloid contained in cacao beans, resembles caffeine in its action, but its effect on the central nervous system is much less powerful, so it can't really be seen as a stimulant. In order to discern any effects, you would have to eat masses, and as we know, too much of anything is bad for you. We must take all this scientific evidence (often cited by chocolate producers) with a pinch of salt and never rely on chocolate alone to replace a healthy balanced diet—view it as a dietary supplement to be taken in moderation and regularly.

Now to dispel a couple of nagging chocolate myths, so that we can appreciate it as a life-enhancing part of our diet. Eating chocolate does not cause acne. The UK Food Standards Agency, the American Dietetic Association, and the American Academy of Dermatology are adamant that there is no link between chocolate and acne. It's all about balance—over-dosing on any food causes imbalance and dietary problems.

Cocoa and chocolate alone do not damage your teeth—what's harmful is usually the high quantity of sugar in poor-quality, mass-produced chocolate bars. In fact, cacao naturally contains fluoride that fights plaque and oral bacteria. Scientific research and pure common sense show us that the fruit of the cacao tree itself isn't harmful to health—it is the addition of too much sugar and vegetable fat to make low-grade chocolate that makes it addictive and heart-stopping.

Purists and chocolate lovers who would like to make the most of chocolate as a health food should try eating raw cacao nibs and cacao pulp. These are both seen to be health-giving natural foods, rich in antioxidants. Cacao nibs can even be used in baking instead of chocolate chips. However, be aware they *will* taste bitter as they are pure cacao bean, so be sure to use them in a recipe containing sugar.

All those who love chocolate know in their hearts that the purer the chocolate, the better it is for you. I recommend a daily prescription of one small square of best-quality dark chocolate, savored slowly first thing in the morning (when the palate is at its freshest), to give yourself a palpable lift, as well as the best possible start to the day. Failing that, keep the whole household happy with my chocolate cakes and teabreads, that just get better for maturing for a day or two in the cake pan. Make a grumpy child happy by baking a batch of Chocolate Brownies or some Chocolate Chip Cookies with them after school. Surprise a down-in-the-dumps friend with a box of homemade Truffles—best shared with a glass of deep, rich red wine or port to help the digestion. Delight dinner guests with dark and mysterious Chocolate Cardamom Truffle Cake or little pots of darkest Chocolate Mousse. Drop round and treat your Mum to a lighter-than-air Chocolate Madeleine over a cup of coffee. There's a recipe for every mood and moment in this book—try one today and you'll feel all the better for it. Chocolate is THE best first aid!

SOUTH AMERICAN ORIGINS AND CHOCOLATE COMES TO EUROPE

Based on pictorial evidence in carvings, paintings, and medieval manuscripts, we know that that the cacao bean was grown and used in tropical pre-Columbian Mesoamerica (Central America) by the Olmecs, Maya, Toltecs, and Aztecs (from whom we get the original name of chocolate—*cacauatl* or *xocolatl*). This takes legendary cocoa as far back as 2000 B.C.

The peoples of Mesoamerica instinctively knew how to get the best out of unpalatable cacao beans to turn them into something appealing. They dried them in the sun, then roasted them, and finally ground them on the traditional three-legged *metate* (grinding stone), heated from beneath by glowing coals. There are paintings of Mayan women kneeling over these sloping *metate* (see picture, right), punishingly grinding away with the rolling pin-like *mano* to produce the butter-wet cocoa liquor used to make their foaming drink, *cacauatl.*

The expansionist Aztecs adopted the cultivation of cacao from the Maya in the fourteenth century and prepared a similar drink, *xocolatl,* where cacao beans were roasted, ground, and mixed with boiling water, ground chiles, and spices to produce a foamy liquid. These drinks, often thickened with maize meal, were considered nourishing, providing essential fats and antioxidants. The best beans were even used as offerings in sacred ceremonies—representing life-blood itself. Both Maya and Aztecs used cacao beans as currency in trading (originally mistaken by Columbus on his first encounter for worthless nuts) and as tribute money and taxes collected from conquered peoples. It was the conspicuous consumption of chocolate by the Aztec elite before the masses that furthered its prestige.

The history of chocolate in Europe begins with the Spanish conquest of Mexico in the sixteenth century and the trade between the two lands. The Spaniards had recognized only the medicinal and health benefits attached to cocoa by the native peoples and took this custom of drinking chocolate back with them to the Spanish court.

The taste for chocolate gradually spread throughout the elite households of Europe. It was made more palatable to European tastes by flavoring it with vanilla, cinnamon, aniseed, chiles, and black pepper, coloring it red with *acciote,* and sweetening it with newly discovered cane sugar. And it was now being served hot, not cold. The foam on top of chocolate was much prized and was produced using a hand-held rotary whisk or *molinillo.* Only the wealthy could afford to drink chocolate, as both cocoa and sugar were expensive imports. Baroque Europe deemed it healthful and it became so fashionable that a vessel called a *mancerina* was invented so that it could be drunk at court without spilling and thus ruining a gown. The French had oblique-handled pots, *chocolatières,* with an integrated wooden *moussoir* and beakers with saucers to catch the drips.

Eventually, Spain and many other mainland European nations established colonial plantations for growing cacao and sugar. For centuries, chocolate remained a handmade luxury. The Spanish learned from the Aztecs how to make a solid, portable, and storable chocolate that could make an instant drink, and this practice of making cakes, balls, or bricks spread rapidly throughout Europe and as far as Samoa, establishing itself as the forerunner of our modern-day chocolate bar.

Chocolate reached Britain in the seventeenth century via Jamaican cacao plantations "liberated" in 1655 by Oliver Cromwell from the Spanish. The drink infiltrated the coffee shops, and anyone who could afford it could drink it—in Britain chocolate had lost the courtly elitism of continental Europe. The English adopted the custom of adding sherry sack, milk, and egg yolks to enrich the drink, and drank it out of shallow bowls. It was through the British colonization of America that chocolate became known again as a drink.

The first European chocolate factory appeared in southwestern France, in Bayonne, in 1761. Then, with the invention in 1778 of the first hydraulic machine for crushing and mixing the chocolate paste, followed in 1819 by the first steam-powered production plant, mass production made solid chocolate affordable to a much broader public. In the nineteenth century, the importance of drinking chocolate declined and solid eating chocolate started to grow in importance and with it the birth of some of the great chocolate dynasties we know today.

Top left: a Samoan chocolate and spice ball, whole and grated

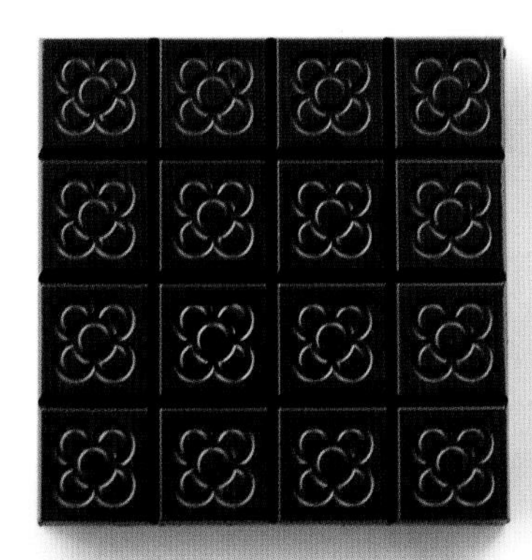

THE CHOCOLATE PROCESS

HOW IT GETS FROM TREE TO BAR

You only have to taste a raw, bland cacao bean to realize what a truly ingenious process it is to turn it into the aromatic chocolate we know today. Tasting a dried cacao bean or a cacao nib will make you wonder what the Spaniards ever saw in the bitter, unpleasant bean in the first place. The chocolate-making process is nothing short of miraculous—pure alchemy!

A FEW CHOCOLATE TERMS EXPLAINED

Cacao tree The tropical tree that produces cacao beans. It was officially classified in 1753 by Swedish scientist Carl von Linnaeus. He deemed cacao so important that he named the tree *Theobroma cacao.* The name derives from the ancient Greek "theos" meaning "god" and "broma" meaning "food." This was added as a prefix to the native name of "cacao."

Cacao pod The fruit of the cacao tree—a leathery oval pod which contains cacao beans and pulp. It is sometimes known as a *cabosse.*

Cacao bean The seed of the cacao tree, which is only called a cacao bean once it is removed from the pod.

Cacao nib The meat of the cacao bean after the shell is removed in the chocolate production process. Cacao nibs sold in health food shops are usually cracked or chopped.

Cocoa liquor Also called cocoa mass, the oily chocolate paste produced by grinding the cacao nibs. It is the basic ingredient in all chocolate products. (It does *not* contain any alcohol.)

Conching Cocoa liquor, cocoa butter, and sugar are blended and placed in large agitators called "conches" that stir and grind the mixture under heat.

Dutch processing or Dutching A method invented by Dutchman C. J. van Houten of treating the cacao nib or cocoa liquor with an alkali solution after roasting. This reduces the acidity in the bean by increasing the pH level from about 5.0 to 8.0.

Let's start by looking at the cacao tree itself. Being tropical, it loves humidity and it will only grow in a thin belt around the equator within the latitudes of 20° South and 20° North. It also needs the shelter of other trees growing around it. Bizarrely, cacao pods grow directly from the trunk of the tree and the larger branches (known as "cauliflory"). The tree is in bloom almost all year round and annually produces around 50,000 flowers. The beautiful, delicate, spidery flowers have no scent and are difficult to pollinate—they are pollinated by a type of midge that only lives under the canopy of the taller trees protecting the cacao trees. The tree matures for 10 years before producing quality fruit and can grow to about 25 feet. Each tree may produce up to 50 pods a year, only giving about 15–20 lb beans in total.

Left: cacao pods in all their vivid colors

Ripe cacao pods are very colorful, ranging from yellow, through orange to red and purple. The pods take about four to eight months to ripen on the tree before harvesting, depending on the variety. Each pod contains about 30 oval-shaped cacao beans surrounded by a slightly sour-sweet fruity pulp. This pulp is delicious and very nutritious in its own right. At this stage if you taste a fresh bean and the pulp, there is absolutely no hint of chocolate! Each cacao bean consists of about 5% water, 54% cocoa butter, 11.5% protein, 9% starch, and many other elements including aromatic oils and small amounts of the stimulants theobromine and caffeine.

BEAN TYPES

There are three types of cacao beans: Criollo, Forastero, and Trinitario.

Criollo are the rarest and most expensive of all cacao beans and are therefore "The King." The name means "native" in Spanish, and was originally discovered by Christopher Columbus in 1502 on the island of Guanaja, Honduras. It is found growing in the rich soil and mild climate of South and Central America. It has a low yield and an extremely fine aroma and low acidity. Nowadays it is often cross-bred with Trinitario for better yields and accounts for 1–4% of the world's production.

Forastero means "foreigner" in Spanish, as the beans were introduced to European-owned plantations in the early twentieth century. They are the most commonly grown cacao bean, are grown mainly in West Africa and the Amazonian Highlands, and make up about 80–90% of the world's production. Although the trees are vigorous and high yielding, the beans lack aroma and tend to be bitter. However, there are always exceptions, and a name often mentioned by professionals in the chocolate industry is Arriba (or Cacao Nacional) from Ecuador. This is a sought-after Forastero bean with a flowery, fruity fragrance which cannot be grown outside Ecuador.

Trinitario beans are believed to be a hybrid of Criollo and Forastero, emerging after disease destroyed most of the native Criollo trees on Trinidad. 30 years later, the Forastero variety was imported and planted on the island. The few remaining Criollo trees began to hybridize with these new trees producing the new variety of Trinitario. The trees are robust and high yielding, with good, aromatic beans. They are grown mainly in Indonesia, Sri Lanka, South America, and the Caribbean Islands. About 10–15% of the world's cocoa production is Trinitario.

FROM PODS TO CHOCOLATE BAR

Although the cacao tree continuously produces flowers and fruit, the main harvesting seasons are November to January and May to July. The harvesting is done very carefully by hand, using machetes, so as not to damage the trunk. Being very susceptible to disease, any damage to the tree would weaken it. Once the pods are harvested, each one is opened by hand and the beans with their surrounding soft pulp are removed. The whole lot is layered in pierced fermentation boxes or baskets between banana leaves. The pulp liquefies and drains out of the bottom of the box and the beans ferment. This generally takes three to seven days. Proper fermentation is the key to developing a full and rounded aroma, and less scrupulous farmers often cut the process out.

Drying The beans must be dried to prolong the shelf life when stored. Their water content is reduced from 60% to about 7% before the beans can be graded and stored. Beans are generally slowly sun-dried or dried in special rooms like giant airing cupboards. The longer the drying process, the better the flavor in the bean. Again, unscrupulous processors speed-dry them over wood fires giving the beans an undesirable smoky flavor that will not disappear. Dried beans are known as "almendras"—the Spanish word for almonds.

Roasting It is careful roasting that really brings out the color and what we all recognize as true chocolate flavor in the bean. Different bean types require different roasting times. Bean types are roasted separately then mixed together when creating a blend.

Winnowing After roasting, the cacao bean shells are removed leaving brittle cacao nibs. The shells are sold for use in medicine and as mulch for gardens.

Grinding The nibs are ground to an oily paste resembling dark brown peanut butter. This is called cocoa liquor (or mass) and only now begins to smell of chocolate. Then, either the cocoa liquor is further pressed, through a process called Dutching, into cocoa butter and cocoa (usually only done with low-quality beans for the mass market) or the liquor is ground again to produce a finer paste to be made into chocolate—both cheap chocolate and expensive chocolate. The cocoa butter is often deodorized to make it more useful to other industries, such as the beauty industry. Good white chocolate is made with nondeodorized cocoa butter.

Conching After the grinding, a process called conching takes place. Other ingredients, such as sugar, extra cocoa butter, powdered milk (for milk chocolate), vanilla, and sometimes the stabilizer lecithin are mixed in, then the cocoa liquor is stirred and mixed at a temperature of about 180°F for between four and 70 hours—less time is required for inferior chocolate. The friction between the sugar crystals and the cacao particles causes further polishing and refining and a chemical change takes place in the mix, giving the chocolate its fullest mellow, ripe, and round flavor and silken smooth texture. The liquid chocolate is then stored in warm tanks until ready for the next stage.

Tempering The chocolate temperature is raised then lowered so that the crystals of cocoa butter re-align and will make the chocolate shiny and crisp when set. Once tempered, the chocolate is poured into molds, which are tapped or shaken to expel any air bubbles trapped in the chocolate, then the molds are cooled, the chocolate tipped out and wrapped. After this, correct storage is all-important or the chocolate could be ruined. Thus the bean finally makes it to the bar—what a magnificent journey it undergoes to become the world's most popular and sublimely harmless fix!

Right: cacao beans

CHOCOLATE TYPES

In essence, there are three familiar types of chocolate, loosely described as dark, milk, and white. However, there has been a revolution in chocolate-making, transforming it into something akin to wine- or olive oil-making. We are now seeing single-bean chocolate, single-estate chocolate, organic chocolate, Fair Trade chocolate, chocolate made in the antique style, with a gritty texture from roughly crushed beans and coarse sugar and flavored with cinnamon or chile, to pure chocolate and spice balls made to be grated into savory dishes or hot drinks. The list is endless, but here are some basic chocolate descriptions to help the home cook.

Dark chocolate contains no powdered milk and has a minimum of 43% cocoa solids (35% in the USA).

Milk chocolate has a minimum of 25% cocoa solids (10% in the USA), is enriched with powdered milk for a creamy, luxurious texture, and has more added sugar.

White chocolate has no cocoa liquor, and is therefore not considered real chocolate, but rather confectionery. It is made from a combination of cocoa butter, sugar, milk solids, and usually flavored with vanilla. The worst is adulterated with other vegetable fats, is flavored with synthetic vanillin, and is very white in color. The best are ivory-colored, have a high cocoa butter percentage, milk solids for creamy richness, and are flavored with real vanilla and may contain lecithin. In the USA it must be called "white confectionery coating." It has a short shelf-life, is a little tricky to work with, and can pick up alien flavors.

Chocolate-flavored cake covering is full of vegetable fat, nothing to do with real chocolate at all, and best avoided.

Couverture (French for "covering") is a special kind of cooking chocolate used by professional chefs. The high cocoa butter content (33–44%) gives a free-flowing, glossy chocolate that handles well. Because of its free-flowing nature, couverture is used for dipping and coating and is often used in chocolate fountains. Not all couverture is ready-tempered. It is useful for baking as it melts easily. It comes in various cocoa mass percentages (dark, milk, and white).

PERCENTAGES EXPLAINED

The difference between varieties of chocolate is in the percentage of cocoa solids. "Cocoa solids" refers to everything that is in a crushed cacao bean, including added cocoa butter. So when the wrapper on a chocolate bar states that it contains 70% cocoa solids, that means that 70% of the bar comes from cacao beans.

Please note, however, that a high percentage of cocoa solids doesn't necessarily mean a strong chocolate flavor: 70% cocoa solids can mean 50% ground beans plus 20% cocoa butter; or 68% ground beans plus 2% cocoa butter. Taste is the only test! The remaining percentage could be sugar, milk, powdered milk, (in the case of milk and white chocolate) vanilla, and maybe some lecithin. 100% cocoa solids means it is all bean and perhaps some cocoa butter.

As a rough guide, a high percentage of cocoa solids coupled with a relatively high price should guarantee quality chocolate, but nothing will beat the taste test. Good chocolate doesn't come cheap. Always look on the label for a percentage of cocoa solids—if it isn't there, then don't buy the chocolate.

AMERICAN CHOCOLATE TYPES

In these days of cross-fertilization of recipes and cookbooks between the UK and USA, it is important to clarify basic chocolate types and their equivalents. Legislation is slightly different, but this should explain things.

Unsweetened or baking chocolate is pure, set cocoa liquor or cocoa solids, very bitter, no sugar.

Bitter, dark, or plain chocolate contains a minimum of 35% cocoa solids, cocoa butter, and sugar.

Extra bitter chocolate can contain up to 70% or more cocoa solids.

Semisweet chocolate contains a minimum of 15–35% cocoa solids, with extra cocoa butter and added sugar.

Sweet cooking chocolate contains the same as above, with more sugar.

Milk chocolate contains cacao solids (about 10–15%), cocoa butter, milk or powdered milk, sugar, and vanilla.

White chocolate—see above.

Decorator's chocolate or confectioner's chocolate is the same as chocolate-flavored cake covering (see page 15).

OTHER CHOCOLATE FORMS

Callets or pistoles are small pellets or flat buttons of chocolate made so that they will melt quickly and evenly. These are mainly used by those in the chocolate trade and come in all three chocolate types. Do not confuse these with mass-produced chocolate drops or chips which are designed to hold their shape when baked, and are not the best chocolate.

Dragées, chocolate balls etc are shaped chocolate. Dragées are almond- or cocoa bean-shaped and covered with edible gold, silver, or any imaginable color of candy coating. They also come in heart forms and balls and are used for decoration.

SOME MODERN TERMS EXPLAINED

Chocolate terminology is constantly evolving, and there is no universal legislation as yet, so here are some explanations of frequently used terms in the world of gourmet chocolate.

Exclusive derivation chocolate is a broad term used to emphasize the variety or unique provenance of the bean.

Estate chocolate is made from beans grown on one plantation, and can be made with more than one variety of bean.

Single-origin and single-variety chocolate refers to chocolate made with cacao beans from one country or region only. It does *not* refer to the quality or type of the bean. Single variety simply means that only cacao beans of one variety have been used. The quality is determined by the type of bean and the chocolate-making process itself.

Grand Cru is a term borrowed from the wine world. It is used to describe high-quality chocolate made from selected cacao beans from particular geographical regions.

CHOCOLATE TIPS

STORING CHOCOLATE

Chocolate and cocoa easily absorb other flavors and odors, so it should be stored tightly wrapped in plastic wrap in an airtight container in a cool, dry place—NOT the fridge, which is too cold and full of moisture. Kept at 50°F, all chocolate should stay in good condition for about a year. If badly stored in hot or humid conditions, the cocoa butter (with rapid temperature change) or the sugar crystals (in the case of humidity) in the chocolate may rise to the surface of the chocolate and become visible as a dull, whitish film, called "bloom." The bloom will not affect the taste and it can still be used perfectly well in baking.

Always bring chocolate to room temperature in its wrapping before cooking. This way it will not attract moisture in the air.

Due to the high proportion of milk solids in white and milk chocolate, they do not keep as well as cocoa and dark chocolate.

Dark, milk, and white chocolate can be frozen providing they are wrapped tightly and thoroughly so that no air can circulate around the surface of the chocolate, thus drawing in moisture. It should be thawed at room temperature, still tightly wrapped. This is really only a good idea if you live in a very hot country.

TO MELT CHOCOLATE ON THE STOVETOP

Break, chop, or grate the chocolate into small, even-size pieces and put it in a clean, dry, thick Pyrex or china basin. The smaller you chop or grate the chocolate, the easier it will be to melt. Fill a saucepan one-quarter full of hot water and bring to a simmer (never let the water boil). Fit the bowl snugly into the rim of the saucepan so that it is suspended over the simmering water, and no steam can escape around the sides. The base of the bowl must not touch the water or the chocolate will overheat.

If melting a small quantity of chocolate, remove the saucepan from the heat and set aside to let the chocolate to melt—this way it will not overheat.

For larger quantities, leave the bowl on the saucepan until the chocolate looks melted—gently prod it with the end of a spoon—it may look solid when it has in fact melted.

When melted, remove the bowl or pan from the heat and stir the chocolate gently until it is completely melted. Stir with a wooden spoon or a plastic spatula rather than a metal one, which may cause bubbles to form and the chocolate to seize.

Do not let the temperature of the chocolate rise above 122°F—a digital or chocolate thermometer is useful for this.

If water or steam comes into contact with the chocolate, the chocolate will seize, go grainy, or turn into a solid mass that will not melt. Do not despair! Pour at least two tablespoons of boiling water into the chocolate and stir gently until the whole mass becomes smooth again. It WILL work but be warned, use this rescued chocolate only for baking—truffle dipping is out!

However, if you melt the chocolate with a lot of water, the chocolate will not seize (see individual recipes).

Always take extra care with white chocolate as it melts at a lower temperature and can easily burn if overheated.

TO MELT CHOCOLATE IN A MICROWAVE OVEN

These are guidelines only. All microwaves have different power outputs. Many factors affect the melting properties of chocolate—amount of cocoa solids, cocoa butter etc, so this is a very rough guide. Err on the cautious side to begin with.

Break or chop the chocolate into small, even-size pieces and put it in a clean, dry Pyrex or china bowl—thicker bowls help reduce the risk of over-heating the chocolate.

For small quantities, put the microwave on a LOW or MEDIUM setting. For larger quantities, and only once you become more experienced, use HIGH.

Check the chocolate frequently and gently prod it with the end of a spoon—it may look solid when in fact it has melted. White chocolate will burn more easily so watch it very carefully—in fact I don't really like melting this in the microwave because of the risk of hot spots.

The addition of other ingredients, such as butter or liquid, may shorten the melting time.

Approximate melting times in a 650 watt microwave oven:

2–4 oz chopped chocolate on 100% power takes about 2 minutes; on 30% power it takes about 5 minutes.

6–8 oz chopped chocolate on 100% power takes about 2–2½ minutes; on 30% power it takes about 6 minutes.

If in doubt, melt the chocolate in 1-minute bursts, giving it a prod every now and then.

SMALL CAKES AND COOKIES

These little cakes are light and airy, with a subtle chocolate flavor and a delicate hint of orange blossom—and they have those little mounds on top showing that they have been perfectly cooked. The secret is in using two oven temperatures—hot then cooler—and buttering and flouring the tins really well to keep the madeleines from sticking.

CHOCOLATE AND ORANGE-BLOSSOM MADELEINES

½ cup plus 1 tablespoon all-purpose flour, plus extra to dust

3 tablespoons unsweetened cocoa

1 teaspoon baking powder

3 large eggs

6 tablespoons granulated sugar

2 tablespoons orange-blossom or acacia honey

1 teaspoon pure vanilla essence

1 teaspoon orange-flower water

5 tablespoons unsalted butter, melted and cooled, plus 3 tablespoons, melted, to grease

a piping bag

two 9-cup metal madeleine molds

MAKES 18 MADELEINES

Sift the flour with the cocoa and baking powder in a small bowl.

In a large bowl, beat the eggs, sugar, honey, vanilla essence, and orange-flower water until pale, thick, and foamy, then fold in the flour mixture. Drizzle the butter around the edge of the bowl and fold it in. Spoon the mixture into the piping bag (there is no need for a tip). Seal the end with a twist of plastic wrap and refrigerate for at least 1 hour or even overnight.

Preheat the oven to 450°F or its hottest setting. Meanwhile, using a pastry brush, liberally grease the molds with butter and refrigerate until set, then dust with flour.

Take the piping bag out of the fridge and pipe the mixture into the molds until very nearly full. Bake for exactly 4 minutes, then turn the heat down to 400°F and bake for a further 4 minutes.

Remove from the oven. Tap the molds sharply on a work surface to loosen the madeleines and let them tumble out. Let cool on a wire rack, then store in an airtight container. Serve with a cup of hot chocolate or Earl Grey tea.

A good, fudgy brownie is hard to beat. Children might prefer these made with a mild dark chocolate or even a good milk chocolate. Make double quantities of this recipe and freeze half of it—you'll be glad you did.

DOUBLE CHOCOLATE AND WALNUT BROWNIES

1½ sticks (12 tablespoons) unsalted butter, softened

2 cups granulated sugar

3 large eggs, beaten

4 oz dark chocolate (60–70% cocoa solids)

1 teaspoon pure vanilla essence

1 cup plus 2 tablespoons all-purpose flour

1 generous cup walnuts, roughly chopped

6½ oz white chocolate chips

a deep 9-inch square baking pan, baselined with waxed or nonstick parchment paper

MAKES 16 BROWNIES

Preheat the oven to 350°F.

Using an electric mixer, cream the butter and sugar together until pale and fluffy, then beat in the eggs. Melt the chocolate according to the instructions on page 17. Stir the melted chocolate and vanilla essence into the butter mixture. Fold in the flour, then the walnuts and half the chocolate chips. Spoon into the prepared baking pan and smooth the surface. Scatter with the remaining chocolate chips (these may brown slightly when baked).

Bake for 30–35 minutes or until a toothpick inserted into the center pulls out with fudgy crumbs attached. Do not overbake as the brownies will continue to cook in the pan when you remove them from the oven. Let cool in the pan—this helps keep the brownies moist. When cold, turn out of the pan, peel off the paper, and cut into 16 squares. Store in an airtight container.

Make these muffins to eat straight out of the oven while the chocolate is still soft and melting—there won't be any left by the end of the day! You could make them using milk instead of sour cream, but the texture won't be as soft and crumbly. Pop a paper muffin case into each muffin pan cup before baking and there will be no washing up.

WARM CHOCOLATE MUFFINS

2 cups plus 2 tablespoons all-purpose flour

3 tablespoons unsweetened cocoa

2½ teaspoons baking powder

½ teaspoon baking soda

6 oz dark chocolate (60–70% cocoa solids), very roughly chopped

3½ oz milk chocolate (over 32% cocoa solids), grated

2 large eggs, beaten

½ cup light brown sugar

1¼ cups sour cream

7 tablespoons unsalted butter, melted

a 12-cup nonstick muffin pan

MAKES 12 MUFFINS

Preheat the oven to 400°F.

Sift the flour, cocoa, baking powder, and baking soda in a large bowl and stir in the chopped and grated chocolates. In a separate bowl, beat together the eggs, sugar, sour cream, and melted butter. Add the liquid mixture to the dry ingredients and stir until just combined and the mixture is fairly stiff. Don't overmix otherwise the muffins will be tough. Spoon the mixture into the muffin pan cups to fill almost to the tops.

Bake for 20 minutes until risen and firm. Leave in the pan for about 15 minutes before turning out as the mixture is quite tender: cakes made with sour cream or buttermilk have a lovely tender crumb. Turn out onto a wire rack and serve warm or cool.

For these little treats, I have taken the basic recipe for one of the most famous chocolate cakes in the world, Viennese Sachertorte, and baked it in small molds. Instead of sandwiching and covering the cakes with apricot jam, I thought a juicy, candied apricot nestling on top of each one would be really exciting. If you are short on time, use real glacé apricots. A glossy coat of luscious chocolate icing finishes off these little Sachertortes perfectly.

LITTLE SACHERTORTES

1 recipe Glossy Chocolate Glaze (page 136)

6½ oz dark chocolate (60–70% cocoa solids)

1 stick (8 tablespoons) unsalted butter, cubed

8 eggs, separated

2 teaspoons pure vanilla essence

a pinch of salt

¾ cup plus 2 tablespoons granulated sugar

1 cup all-purpose flour

CANDIED APRICOTS (MAKES ABOUT 10 OZ)

1 cup plus 1 tablespoon sugar

2 tablespoons light corn syrup

8 oz dried apricots (at least 24)

vegetable oil, to grease

12 dariole molds or custard cups

MAKES 12 SACHERTORTES

To make the candied apricots, put the sugar and corn syrup in a heavy-based, wide pan, (at least 3 inches deep) with ¾ cup water. Heat gently, stirring occasionally, for about 10 minutes, or until the sugar has completely dissolved. Add the apricots, then turn up the heat and bring to a boil. Turn down the heat to a gentle simmer and cook, uncovered, until the apricots are slightly plump and glassy—about 25 minutes. Baste and turn them occasionally. Remove the pan from the heat, cover tightly, and let stand for 20 minutes or even overnight to plump up the fruit.

Grease a wire rack lightly with vegetable oil and set on top of a tray or baking sheet. Lift the apricots out of the syrup with a slotted spoon and set on the rack to drain and cool. Reserve the syrup. When the apricots are cold, layer between sheets of parchment paper in an airtight container. Refrigerate for up to 1 month.

Preheat the oven to 350°F. Butter and flour the dariole molds and line the bases with circles of nonstick parchment paper.

To make the cake batter, melt the chocolate with the butter according to the instructions on page 17. Lightly beat the egg yolks, then add them to the chocolate mixture with the vanilla essence and beat until smooth.

Using an electric mixer, beat the egg whites with the salt in a clean, dry bowl until they form stiff peaks, then gradually beat in the sugar to make a stiff meringue mixture. Fold a tablespoon of the meringue into the chocolate mixture with a metal spoon to loosen it, then fold in the rest. Sift the flour on top and fold in gently. Spoon the batter into the molds and tap gently on the table to settle the mixture. Put them on a baking sheet and bake for 20–25 minutes, or until a skewer inserted in the center comes out clean. Remove from the oven and let cool in the molds. When cool, slice off any cake that has risen above the mold to make a flat base. Invert onto a wire rack set on top of a tray, and brush with the reserved apricot syrup.

Place two small (or one large) candied apricots on top of each Sachertorte, then spoon the Glossy Chocolate Glaze over each one to cover completely. Refrigerate for 30 minutes to set. Serve at room temperature.

These are my favorite cakes from a French pâtisserie. *I often buy one and take it to a café to eat with a steaming cup of coffee—almost a religious experience! Follow my instructions below for perfect choux pastry. Weigh and measure everything exactly, sift the flour well, and don't boil the liquid until the butter has melted. Add the beaten egg gradually: too little and the pastry will not rise properly, too much and the pastry will collapse. The choux buns must dry out completely before filling, so returning them to the oven once pierced will help. Sometimes these are piped decoratively with buttercream icing, but I prefer them quite plain. Once cool, the buns can be used immediately, stored in an airtight container, or frozen.*

RELIGIEUSES AU CHOCOLAT

1 recipe Chocolate Crème Pâtissière (page 137), at room temperature

½ recipe Glossy Chocolate Glaze (page 136), warmed

1¼ cups all-purpose flour

a good pinch of salt

1 stick (8 tablespoons) unsalted butter, cubed

½ cup milk

4 medium eggs, beaten

a piping bag fitted with a plain, medium tip

MAKES 6 RELIGIEUSES

Preheat the oven to 375°F.

Sift the flour with the salt twice onto a large sheet of waxed paper.

Put the butter in a heavy-based pan with the milk and ½ cup water and heat slowly. The liquid must not boil until the butter has completely melted. Once at a rolling boil, pour in the flour all at once, remove the pan from the heat, and beat well until all the lumps are gone and the mixture JUST begins to pull away from the sides of the pan. Do not overbeat or the mixture will become heavy and greasy.

Let cool for 5 minutes, then using an electric mixer or a food mixer, gradually beat in the eggs, until thickened and glossy. Beat well between each addition—the more you beat at this stage, the lighter the pastry will be. You may not have to add all the egg. The mixture is ready when it is smooth and shiny, still holds its shape, and will reluctantly leave the spoon when tapped. Spoon into the piping bag.

Wet two heavy baking sheets and pipe 6 walnut-size mounds of choux onto one and 6 larger mounds, about 2 inches in diameter, onto the other, spacing the mounds well apart.

Bake for 20–25 minutes for the smaller choux and 35 minutes for the larger ones. They should look well puffed and golden brown. Remove from the oven and make a large hole in the base of each one with the tip of a knife. Replace on the baking sheets and return to the oven for a further 5 minutes to dry out the insides. Let cool on a wire rack.

Put the Chocolate Crème Pâtissière into a clean piping bag and pipe into the base hole of each choux. Dip the tops of the filled choux buns into the warm Glossy Chocolate Glaze and leave for 5 minutes to set. Sit each small choux on top of a larger one. You may like to trim the base from the smaller ones to ensure a good fit! Eat immediately before they become soggy.

These are large, flat cookies, perfect for sandwiching together with ice cream. To make smaller ones for eating with malted milk or a milkshake, use smaller spoonfuls and don't spread the mixture out. Although real chopped chocolate tastes better, it won't hold its shape as nicely as ready-made chocolate chips. For real chocoholics, use cacao nibs instead.

DOUBLE CHOCOLATE CHIP COOKIES

5 tablespoons unsalted butter, softened
5 tablespoons granulated sugar
5 tablespoons light brown sugar, sifted
1 large egg, beaten
½ teaspoon pure vanilla essence or chocolate extract (see note)
1 cup plus 2 tablespoons self-rising flour
3 tablespoons unsweetened cocoa
¼ teaspoon salt
⅔ cup (or more) dark and white (or milk) chocolate chips (or roughly chopped chocolate)

a heavy, nonstick baking sheet

MAKES ABOUT 12 LARGE COOKIES

Preheat the oven to 350°F.

Using an electric mixer, cream the butter and sugars together until pale and fluffy. Beat in the egg and vanilla essence.

Sift the flour with the cocoa and salt in a small bowl. Fold into the egg mixture with the chocolate chips.

Place 4 heaping tablespoonfuls of the mixture on the prepared baking sheet, spacing them well apart. Press down and spread out to about ¼ inch thick with the back of a wet spoon or with dampened fingers (you may like to scatter some more chocolate chips over the top). Bake for 10–12 minutes. Let cool on the baking sheet for 1 minute, then transfer to a wire rack. When cool, store in an airtight container. Repeat with the remaining mixture.

Note: Chocolate extract is a fat-free flavoring ingredient made from a blend of roasted cacao beans, water, and alcohol. Star Kay White's Pure Chocolate Extract is available at www.deandeluca.com or by calling Dean & Deluca on 800-221-7714.

Ballet dancer Anna Pavlova and opera singer Dame Nellie Melba were so loved by their public that both had sweet dishes named after them. Actress Sarah Bernhardt captured hearts wherever she appeared and was similarly honored by a Danish chef who concocted and named these delectable cakes in her honor.

SARAH BERNHARDT CAKES

2 recipes Chocolate Ganache (page 136), at room temperature

1 recipe Glossy Chocolate Glaze (page 136)

⅔ cup ground almonds

½ cup granulated sugar

1 large egg white, lightly beaten

½ teaspoon bitter almond essence

gold leaf or finely chopped pistachios, to decorate

a heavy baking sheet, lined with nonstick parchment paper

a piping bag fitted with a plain, ¼-inch tip

MAKES 20 CAKES

Put the ground almonds and sugar in a blender and process until finely ground. Tip into a bowl and beat in the egg white and almond essence until you get a smooth, workable paste.

Put the mixture into the piping bag and pipe twenty 1⅝-inch mounds onto the prepared baking sheet, spacing them at least 1 inch apart. Let stand for 30 minutes.

Preheat the oven to 300°F.

Bake the macaroons for about 20 minutes, or until they turn pale beige. Slip the paper and macaroons onto a wire rack to cool. When cool, lift the macaroons off the paper and store in an airtight container for up to 3 days.

Beat the Chocolate Ganache until the colour lightens and it becomes stiff enough to hold its shape. Do not overbeat. Spoon the ganache into a clean piping bag and tip. Pipe a 2-inch high teardrop on top of each macaroon, covering the base completely. Chill (or even freeze) for at least 1 hour.

Strain the Glossy Chocolate Glaze through a fine strainer to remove any bubbles. Let cool until almost cold but still runny—about 30 minutes. Pour into a warm wide-necked pitcher or deep bowl. Holding the cake by the base, dip the chilled ganache part quickly and evenly into the glaze. The glaze should cover the join between the ganache and macaroon. Sit each cake on its base, then sprinkle with flecks of gold leaf or finely chopped pistachios. Cover and refrigerate until ready to serve. These can be made up to 2 days in advance.

The ultimate indulgence when visiting Paris is to visit Ladurée and order tea and a silver plate of their exquisite signature macaroons. They come in every flavor imaginable and are crisp on the outside and soft in the center. Everyone has a favorite, and I have mixed and matched two of mine to make a very pretty macaroon indeed—raspberry and chocolate go particularly well together.

CHOCOLATE MACAROONS WITH RASPBERRY BUTTERCREAM

¼ recipe Raspberry Buttercream (page 138)
1¾ cups confectioners' sugar, sifted
scant 1 cup ground almonds
3 tablespoons unsweetened cocoa
4 egg whites
a tiny pinch of salt

two heavy baking sheets, lined with nonstick parchment paper
a piping bag and plain tips (size 10 or 12)

MAKES APPROXIMATELY
10 LARGE MACAROONS OR
40 SMALL MACAROONS

Preheat the oven to 400°F.

Put the confectioners' sugar, ground almonds, and cocoa in a blender or spice grinder and process for about 1 minute to refine the almonds and combine everything.

Using an electric mixer, beat the egg whites with the salt in a clean, dry bowl until firm. Using a large metal spoon, gently fold in the almond mixture.

Carefully spoon the mixture into the piping bag fitted with the size 10 tip (for small macaroons) or the size 12 (for larger macaroons). Pipe twenty 2½-inch macaroons or eighty 1¼-inch ones onto the prepared baking sheets.

Bake with the oven door slightly ajar (to allow steam to escape) for about 8 minutes for the small macaroons or 12 minutes for the larger ones. Don't overcook or they won't be soft inside.

Carefully lift the macaroons off the paper and let cool on a wire rack.

Sandwich in pairs with a thin layer of Raspberry Buttercream. Arrange the macaroons in layers between aluminum foil or parchment paper in an airtight container and refrigerate for 24 hours before serving. This will help them become chewy. Bring to room temperature before serving.

These little meringues make a lovely display for a special tea or piled high instead of a birthday cake. Bright green shelled and shredded pistachios are available from Middle Eastern stores—buy them if you see them and store them in a container in the freezer and they will stay fresh for months.

CHOCOLATE AND PISTACHIO MERINGUES

3 egg whites
a tiny pinch of salt
1 cup confectioners' sugar, sifted
2 teaspoons unsweetened cocoa, sifted
5 oz dark chocolate, 1½ oz of it grated
ground or shredded pistachios, to decorate

PISTACHIO CREAM

3½ oz white chocolate, broken into pieces
3 tablespoons heavy cream
⅓ cup shelled pistachios, finely ground

two heavy baking sheets, lined with nonstick parchment paper
a piping bag fitted with a plain or fluted tip (optional)

MAKES 30 MERINGUES

Preheat the oven to 275°F.

To make the meringues, beat the egg whites with the salt in a clean, dry bowl until quite firm. Gradually beat in the confectioners' sugar, 1 tablespoon at a time, making sure the meringue is as firm as possible between each addition of sugar. Mix the cocoa into the last tablespoon of sugar and beat into the meringue. Quickly fold in the grated chocolate.

Either spoon tablespoons of the meringue onto the prepared baking sheets or fill the piping bag with the mixture and pipe in mounds or rosettes. Bake for 40 minutes, then switch off the oven and let cool in the oven. When cold, carefully lift the meringues off the paper and store for up to 1 week in an airtight container.

To make the pistachio cream, put the white chocolate and cream in a small bowl and set over a pan of simmering water (making sure the bowl does not touch the water). Remove from the heat and set aside to melt. Stir to combine, then let cool for five minutes. Stir in the ground pistachios, then let cool completely but don't refrigerate or the mixture will set too hard.

Melt the remaining chocolate according to the instructions on page 17. Dip the base of each meringue into the melted chocolate and leave on waxed paper to set. To assemble the meringues, sandwich pairs of meringues together with a little pistachio cream, then roll the meringue in the ground or shredded pistachios so that they stick to the cream.

This has always been a great favorite of mine when I want to bake a dessert in advance. Everybody loves the contrast of the crunchy shell and the soft, slightly chewy center. Due to the high fat content of the chocolate, this meringue tends to collapse and spread more than a true pavlova (see my trick below). Strawberries and chocolate are one of those great combinations, and for those who love white chocolate, this is an ideal time to indulge in white chocolate sauce. Keep the cooled meringue in an airtight container until ready to use. You can make this up to 1 day ahead.

CHOCOLATE AND STRAWBERRY PAVLOVA

1 recipe Bitter Chocolate Sauce or Rich Chocolate Fudge Sauce (page 135), warmed

4 large egg whites

a pinch of salt

1 cup superfine sugar, plus extra to taste

1 teaspoon cornstarch

1 tablespoon unsweetened cocoa

1 teaspoon pure vanilla essence

1 teaspoon white wine vinegar

4 oz dark chocolate (60–70% cocoa solids), grated

1¾ cups heavy cream

3 cups strawberries, hulled

a large baking sheet, lined with nonstick parchment paper on which a 9-inch circle has been drawn

SERVES 6

Preheat the oven to 275°F.

Using an electric mixer, beat the egg whites with the salt in a clean, dry bowl until very stiff. Gradually beat in the sugar, 1 tablespoon at a time, making sure the meringue is "bouncily" stiff between each addition of sugar. Beat the cornstarch, cocoa, vanilla essence, and vinegar into the egg whites, then fold in the grated chocolate.

Spoon the meringue onto the marked circle right to the edges—the meringue will spread to approximately 12 inches as it bakes. Bake for about 45 minutes until it is beginning to turn pale brown and has collapsed a little. Remove from the oven and let cool.

Whip the cream to soft peaks with a little sugar to taste. Carefully peel the paper from the pavlova. Cut the pavlova into six wedges and arrange them on a large plate, slightly overlapping the slices—once covered with cream it will look like a real pavlova! Spread out the cream generously and pile the strawberries on top. Serve immediately, drizzled with the Chocolate Sauce.

THE SWISS AND CHOCOLATE

The word "Swiss" has almost become synonymous with chocolate. Thanks to the Swiss, chocolate evolved to become a creamy, mouthwatering confectionery loved the world over. Picture the idyllic white-capped mountain peaks of Switzerland, dotted with grazing cows and you are close to the magic ingredient that changed chocolate forever—milk.

François Louis Cailler (1796–1852) is credited with putting the Swiss on the chocolate map. He opened the first Swiss chocolate factory in 1819 at Corsier, near his home town of Vevey on Lake Geneva. Cailler had learned the art of chocolate-making just next door in Northern Italy, in the very factory that that first produced the infamous chocolate and nut combination, *gianduja*. Cailler invented specialist machinery and began to make chocolate. However, this was not the silken, refined Swiss chocolate we know today, but rather rough, gritty, bitter chocolate. Cacao nibs were ground to the cocoa liquor stage, then pressed further to produce cocoa butter. This was pressed into a mold and left to set, resulting in the very basic chocolate used for making the drink.

Things started to change fast. Philippe Suchard (1797–1874) saw at a young age that chocolate-making might be quite a profitable career since chocolate was considered a luxury item, despite being easy to produce. So, in 1826, Suchard started one of the most famous chocolate dynasties in Switzerland using machinery he had designed himself—the stalwart *mélangeur* or mixing machine.

Now we are getting closer to the birth of Swiss milk chocolate. Milk had never been mixed with chocolate before, since the traditional way to make it was with water.

In 1867, a Swiss chemist called Henri Nestlé (1814–1890) discovered how to dry milk by evaporation. This would prove to be invaluable for new mothers in a world without proper refrigeration. Later, yet another Swiss chocolate manufacturer, called Daniel Peter (1836–1919), had the idea of combining this new powdered milk with cocoa liquor to produce a new, creamy kind of chocolate, and in 1879, the first bar of milk chocolate was produced.

In the very same year, Rodolphe Lindt (1855–1909) invented the technique of "conching" (see page 12), which would improve the quality and texture of chocolate forever. This gave Swiss chocolate its characteristic silky smoothness. The name of Lindt's machine, "conche," is supposedly derived from the Latin word for its shell-like shape. A traditional conche is simply a very efficient grinder that grinds the delicate and volatile beans into an incredibly smooth paste, surrounding each cacao molecule with a coating of cocoa butter. The action of conching creates heat in the mix and gives it a characteristic Swiss "cooked" flavor and super-smooth texture. Extra cocoa butter was added along with the milk powder. The familiar bar that can be snapped and yet melts in the mouth was born. Lindt named this luxuriant eating chocolate "fondant" and it became the world's favorite chocolate. The conche was universally adopted, and chocolate gained the silky texture we know and love today.

During this era of innovation and invention came the discovery of tempering. Cocoa butter in the cocoa liquor often crystallized and ruined the glossy smooth surface of the chocolate. Tempering meant heating cocoa liquor with a high cocoa butter content to a specific temperature, then carefully lowering the temperature. The crystal structure of the cocoa butter shattered, producing a more free-flowing chocolate that could be used for coating or molding, setting hard with a lovely sheen.

In the 24 years between 1890 and 1914, Swiss chocolate exports rocketed from just over 1 million lb to 37 million lb—it had multiplied almost 30 times and represented 55% of total world sales.

So we can truly thank the Swiss for developing the luxurious refined chocolate beloved of all children and young-at-heart. Even dark Swiss chocolate has that incredible smooth melting texture about it.

But then, in 1899, Jean Tobler began marketing his famous triangular, mountain-shaped "Toblerone," speckled with almond and honey nougat (see my homage ice cream recipe on page 94) and companies like Nestlé and Suchard became world players, synonymous with quality chocolate. Today the Swiss are the greatest consumers of chocolate in the world, consuming about 26 lb per capita.

Right: the essential ingredients that first set Swiss chocolate apart from its forerunners: milk, powdered milk, and cocoa butter

CAKES AND TEABREADS

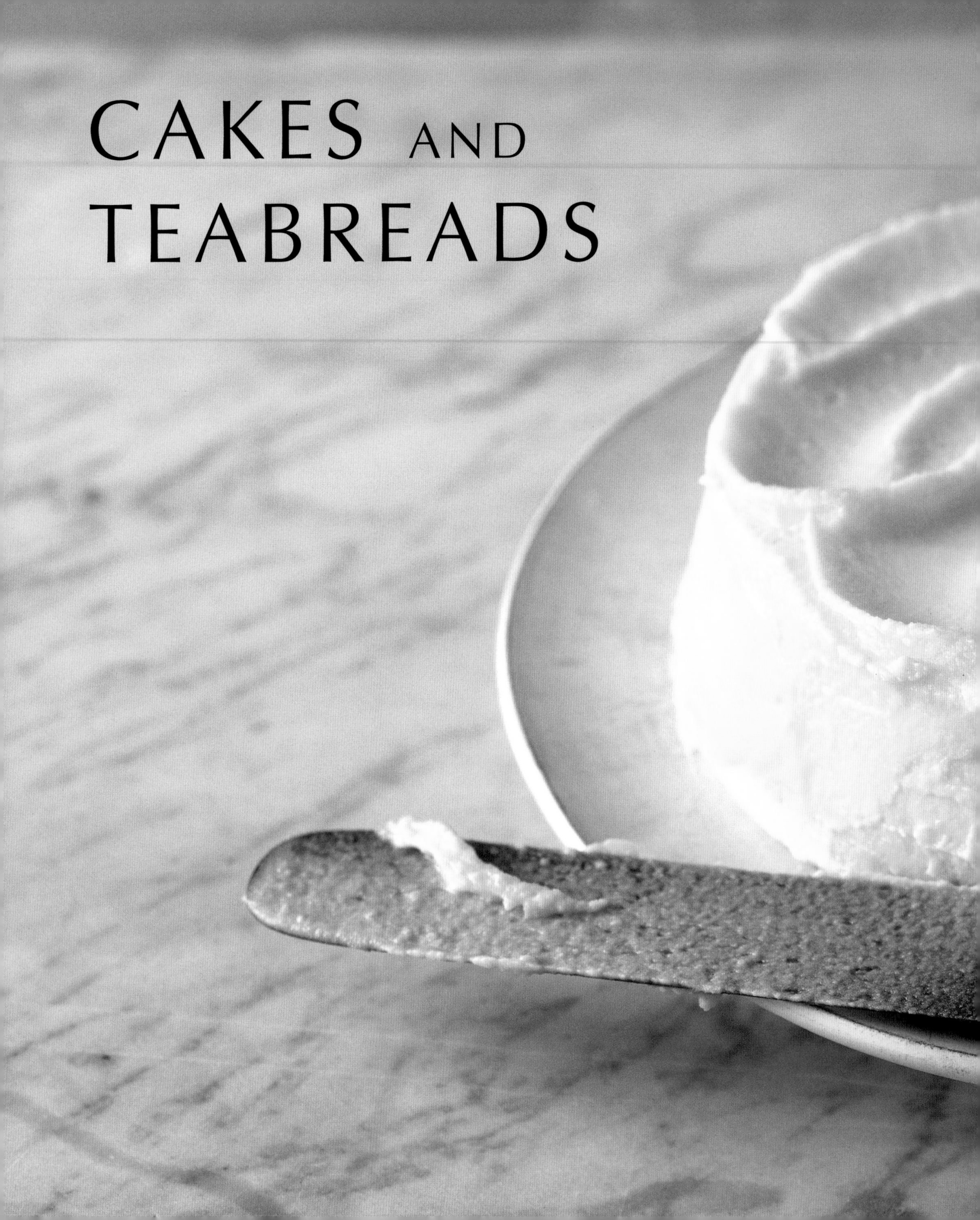

There's something about the combination of really dark chocolate and bitter cherries that is beguiling. These moist little teabreads are studded with those succulent cherries in syrup often found spooned over ice cream in Italian ice cream parlors. More often than not they are sold in lovely blue-and-white jars, but I seek out the cheaper clear jars from Italian specialty stores. Creamy white macadamia nuts are full of oil that can turn rancid very quickly, so don't let them hang around the pantry for too long—use them in these teabreads instead.

CHOCOLATE, CHERRY, AND MACADAMIA TEABREADS

2⅓ cups all-purpose flour

6 tablespoons unsweetened cocoa

1 tablespoon baking powder

½ teaspoon baking soda

½ teaspoon salt

1⅓ cups milk

⅔ cup amarena cherries, plus 6 tablespoons of their syrup

⅓ cup light brown sugar

3 tablespoons unsalted butter, softened

3½ oz dark chocolate (60–70% cocoa solids), broken into pieces

1 cup macadamia nuts, roughly chopped, plus extra to scatter

eight mini loaf pans or two 8 x 4 x 3-inch loaf pans

MAKES 8 MINI TEABREADS OR 2 LARGE TEABREADS

Preheat the oven to 300°F. Grease the loaf pans, baseline with nonstick parchment paper, and dust with flour.

Sift the flour, cocoa, baking powder, baking soda, and salt together in a large bowl.

Heat the milk, amarena cherry syrup, sugar, butter, and chocolate together in a medium pan until melted and smooth. Stir this into the flour mixture as quickly and deftly as possible until just combined—as if you were making muffins. Stir in the cherries and macadamia nuts, then spoon into the pans and smooth the surface. Scatter with extra macadamia nuts.

Bake for about 30 minutes for the smaller pans and 1 hour for the larger pans, or until firm. A metal skewer inserted into the center should come out clean. Remove from the oven and let cool in the pans for 10 minutes. Turn out onto a wire rack and let cool completely. Store in an airtight container for 1 day to mature before serving.

Note: Amarena cherries are available at www.markethallfoods.com or by calling Market Hall Foods at 888-952-4005.

This is a real treat for children everywhere or the big kid that lurks in all of us. I like to use milk chocolate and a flavored yogurt for children or really dark chocolate and natural yogurt for adults. This really does improve with keeping—even for a day—but I can never keep my hands off it. I employ the "stealthy sliver method," and before I know it, it has all gone!

CHOCOLATE AND BANANA BREAD

3½ tablespoons unsalted butter, softened

¾ cup light brown sugar

2 large eggs, beaten

6 tablespoons natural, banana, or chocolate yogurt

2 ripe bananas, mashed

2⅓ cups self-rising flour

½ teaspoon salt

6½ oz dark chocolate (60–70% cocoa solids) or milk chocolate (over 32% cocoa solids), grated

chocolate and hazelnut spread, to serve (optional)

two 8 x 4 x 3-inch loaf pans

MAKES 2 LOAVES

Preheat the oven to 350°F. Grease the loaf pans, baseline with nonstick parchment paper, and dust with flour.

Using an electric mixer, beat the butter and sugar together until well mixed (it won't look very creamy). Gradually beat in the eggs, little by little, then the yogurt, and finally stir in the mashed bananas. Fold in the flour and salt, then the grated chocolate. Spoon into the pans and smooth the surface.

Bake for about 35 minutes, or until risen and firm. It will crack on the top. A metal skewer inserted into the center should come out clean. Remove from the oven and let cool in the pan for 10 minutes. Turn out onto a wire rack and let cool completely. Store in an airtight container for 1 day to mature before serving in thick slices with chocolate and hazelnut spread if you're feeling particularly indulgent!

My first taste of this rich, buttery cake was in the candy-pink, marbled interior of an Austrian coffee shop in the fairytale city of Salzburg. These cakes are piled high in cake shop windows and have that distinctive rounded wobbly base. The marbling effect is easy to achieve—just dollop in large spoonfuls of each mixture randomly and the effect will bake through the cake. And in case you are wondering, two tablespoons of cocoa is plenty—it is very dark when baked.

MARBLED BUTTER KUGELHOPF

14 tablespoons unsalted butter, softened
1 cup granulated sugar
3 large eggs, beaten
⅓ cup milk
1⅔ cups all-purpose flour
1 teaspoon baking powder
2 tablespoons unsweetened cocoa
confectioners' sugar, to dust

an 8-inch kugelhopf mold, greased and dusted with flour

SERVES 6–8

Preheat the oven to 350°F.

Using an electric mixer, beat the butter and sugar together in a large bowl until pale and fluffy. Add the eggs little by little, beating well between each addition. Beat in the milk.

Sift the flour and baking powder together onto a sheet of waxed paper, then pour it into the creamed mixture and beat until smooth.

Divide the batter in half. Beat the cocoa into one half of the batter. Spoon alternate large spoonfuls of batter into the prepared kugelhopf mold. Smooth the surface.

Bake for 50–60 minutes, or until the cake springs back when gently pressed in the middle. Remove from the oven and let cool in the mold for 10 minutes. Turn out onto a wire rack and let cool completely. Dust the top of the kugelhopf generously with confectioners' sugar.

For ginger fans only! Chocolate and ginger is one of the best flavor combinations I know. If you are making this for a really decadent treat, use chocolate-coated stem ginger instead of the usual pieces in syrup, and don't cut them up—when the gingerbread is cooked and sliced you will reveal glowing chunks of ginger enrobed with chocolate. Keep it in a tin for a couple of days to give the gingerbread its stickiness. For special occasions I scatter the top with pieces of crystallized ginger.

STICKY CHOCOLATE GINGERBREAD

2⅓ cups dark molasses

6 oz dark chocolate (60–70% cocoa solids), grated

1¾ cups all-purpose flour

2 teaspoons ground ginger

a pinch of salt

5 oz whole pieces preserved stem ginger, drained and roughly chopped

1 stick (8 tablespoons) unsalted butter, softened

½ cup plus 2 tablespoons dark brown sugar, sifted (to remove lumps)

2 medium eggs, beaten

½ teaspoon baking soda

2 tablespoons milk, warmed

extra-large crystallized ginger pieces, to scatter (optional)

a deep 8-inch square cake pan or 8 x 6 x 3-inch oval cake pan

MAKES AN 8-INCH CAKE

Preheat the oven to 325°F. Grease and line the base and sides of the cake pan with nonstick parchment paper.

Put the molasses in a pan and heat gently until hot, but do not allow it to boil. Remove the pan from the heat and add the chocolate. Stir until melted.

Sift the flour, ground ginger, and salt together in a bowl. Add the stem ginger and toss it around in the flour until every piece is coated.

Using an electric mixer, cream the butter and sugar in a large bowl. Beat in the eggs, then the molasses and chocolate mixture, and finally the flour mixture. Dissolve the baking soda in the milk and gradually beat this into the batter.

Pour into the prepared cake pan, scatter with the crystallized ginger, if using, and bake for 45 minutes. Reduce the oven temperature to 300°F and bake for a further 30 minutes. (If using the oval pan, cook for about 45 minutes at the higher temperature, then about 1 hour at the lower temperature as it will be deeper.) A metal skewer inserted into the center should come out clean. Let cool for 5 minutes in the pan, then turn out onto a wire rack and let cool completely. When cold, store in an airtight container for at least a couple of days to mature and become sticky. Don't worry if it sinks a bit in the middle—this is normal.

I have always wanted to make devil's food cake really devilish by adding the warmth of hot peppers to the cake batter and icing. I tasted all sorts of chile-chocolate combinations and found pasilla chile (also known as "little raisin") to be the best match. It was mild and fruity and the baked cake became strangely addictive. I couldn't resist making candied fresh chiles for the red devil horn decorations—very edible if a little hot!

DEVIL'S FOOD CAKE WITH CHILE FUDGE ICING

6½ oz dark chocolate (60–70% cocoa solids)

14 tablespoons unsalted butter, softened

1¾ cups dark brown sugar

3 eggs, beaten

2⅔ cups self-rising flour

2 tablespoons unsweetened cocoa

2 tablespoons pasilla chile powder (see page 143)

¾ cup sour cream

CANDIED CHILE HORNS

2¼ cups sugar

20 fresh long red chiles

CHILE FUDGE ICING

6½ tablespoons unsalted butter, cubed

1¼ cups light brown sugar

5 oz dark chocolate (60–70% cocoa solids), broken into pieces

1 tablespoon pasilla chile powder (see page 143)

4 tablespoons light cream

2⅓ cups confectioners' sugar, sifted

two deep 8-inch cake pans

SERVES 8–12

To make the candied chile horns, put the sugar and 2⅓ cups water in a large pan. Bring to a boil for 1 minute. Pierce each chile near the stalk end and add to the sugar syrup. Bring to a boil, then turn down the heat and simmer for 45 minutes, or until the chiles are translucent and the syrup looks thick and reduced. Turn off the heat and let soak in the syrup for 24 hours, if possible. Lift the chiles out of the syrup with a fork, drain well, and arrange on nonstick parchment paper. Store in layers in an airtight container for up to 1 month.

Preheat the oven to 350°F.

Lightly grease the cake pans, dust with flour, and baseline with nonstick parchment paper.

To make the cake, melt the chocolate with ⅔ cup water according to the instructions on page 17. Using an electric mixer, cream the butter and sugar in a large bowl until light and fluffy, then gradually beat in the eggs. Beat in the chocolate mixture. Sift the flour, cocoa, and chile powder onto the mixture and fold in. Fold in the sour cream until smooth. Spoon the batter into the prepared pans and bake for about 30 minutes, or until the cakes begin to wrinkle at the sides of the pans and a skewer inserted into the center comes out clean. Remove the cakes from the oven and let cool completely in the pans. Turn out and remove the paper. With a serrated knife, slice each cake in half horizontally.

To make the chile fudge icing, put the butter, brown sugar, chocolate, chile powder, and cream in a medium pan. Heat very gently, without boiling, until melted and dissolved, then bring to a rolling boil and boil for 3 minutes. Remove from the heat and carefully beat in the confectioners' sugar. Beat well until smooth and thick enough to spread—about 2 minutes. Working quickly, sandwich some icing between layers of cake and pile into a high tower, then spread the remaining icing all over the top and sides.

Trim the candied chiles into 2½-inch lengths and push into the icing around the top rim of the cake. It may be tricky to cut, but it looks fabulous!

An oldie but a goodie—you never really tire of this moist, rich chocolate dessert. It is really a cooked chocolate mousse, and without a hint of flour. Covering the roulade with a damp kitchen towel stops it from drying as it cools, keeping it moist and squashy. Serve with the orange compote.

ORANGE CHOCOLATE ROULADE

4 tablespoons orange liqueur

confectioners' sugar and granulated sugar, to dust

1¼ cups heavy cream

ORANGE CHOCOLATE ROULADE

7½ oz dark chocolate (60–70% cocoa solids)

1 teaspoon instant coffee granules

finely grated peel of 1 unwaxed orange (reserving the orange)

5 large eggs, separated

¾ cup sugar

CANDIED PEEL

3 large, firm unwaxed oranges (if you can only get waxed, scrub them in hot soapy water before using)

½ cup sugar

a 9 x 13-inch jelly roll pan, lined with nonstick parchment paper

SERVES 6

Preheat the oven to 425°F.

To make the orange chocolate roulade, melt the chocolate with the coffee and orange peel and 4 tablespoons water, according to the instructions on page 17. Stir until smooth. Beat the egg yolks and sugar in a large bowl until pale and light. Stir in the chocolate mixture. Using an electric mixer, beat the egg whites in a clean, dry bowl until stiff but not dry and fold into the chocolate mixture using a metal spoon. Pour into the prepared pan and spread evenly. Bake for 12–15 minutes, or until risen and firm but not dry. Remove from the oven, cover with a damp kitchen towel, and let cool in the pan.

To make the candied peel, pare the peel from the oranges in long curling strips, leaving behind any bitter white pith. Reserve the oranges. Blanch the peel in a small pan of boiling water for about 2 minutes, then drain. Put the sugar and ¾ cup water in a small pan and heat until the sugar has dissolved. Bring to a boil, then boil for 1 minute. Add the peel and simmer for 25 minutes until it is opaque and the syrup is reduced. Lift out the peel with a fork and let dry on a wire rack set over some paper towels. Reserve the syrup.

To make the orange compote, cut away the pith and peel from the 4 oranges you have reserved and cut out the segments in between the membrane. Put these in a bowl with the orange liqueur and reserved syrup. Stir, cover, and refrigerate until needed.

Dust a large sheet of waxed paper with confectioners' sugar and granulated sugar and turn the baked roulade out onto it. Peel the lining paper away and trim the edges of the roulade to neaten. Whip the cream softly and spread over the roulade. Roll up from the shorter side. Don't worry if it cracks—this is normal and just makes it look better! Lift the roulade onto a serving plate. Dust with extra confectioners' sugar and granulated sugar. Decorate with the candied orange peel and chill until ready to serve with the orange compote.

This romantically named classic French cake is all that you expect the enigmatic Queen of Sheba, who stole the heart of King Solomon, to have been—rich, dark, and tempting. Veiled in darkest cocoa, adorned with gold dragées, and strewn with deep geranium petals, the cake reveals a soft, moist center—what more can I say? On the practical side, don't overcook the cake otherwise it will be too dry.

QUEEN OF SHEBA CHOCOLATE AND ALMOND CAKE

3½ oz dark chocolate (60–70% cocoa solids)
6½ tablespoons unsalted butter, softened
½ cup sugar, plus 1 tablespoon
2 tablespoons rum or coffee
¼ teaspoon bitter almond essence
3 eggs, separated
½ cup ground almonds
a pinch of salt
⅓ cup all-purpose flour
2 tablespoons unsweetened cocoa, plus extra to dust
golden chocolate dragées, to decorate
fresh geranium petals, to decorate

an 8-inch regular or springform cake pan, about 1¼ inches deep

SERVES 6–8

Preheat the oven to 350°F. Grease the cake pan, baseline with nonstick parchment paper, and dust with flour.

Melt the chocolate according to the instructions on page 17. Using an electric mixer, cream the butter and sugar in a large bowl until really pale and fluffy, then beat in the rum and almond essence followed by the egg yolks, one by one. Working quickly, fold the melted chocolate into the egg mixture, then stir in the ground almonds.

Using an electric mixer with clean beaters, beat the egg whites with the salt in a clean, dry bowl until they form floppy peaks, then sprinkle in the remaining tablespoon of sugar and beat again until the mixture forms stiff peaks. Beat a spoonful into the chocolate mixture with a metal spoon to loosen it, then fold in half of the egg whites. Sift the flour and cocoa onto the mixture, then gently fold in. Finally, fold in the remaining egg whites.

Pour the mixture into the cake pan, spreading it out evenly over the base. Bake for 20–25 minutes. Check it after 20 minutes—the cake should be risen and a bit wobbly in the center, but firm around the edges. Remove from the oven and let cool in the pan for 10 minutes. Loosen the sides with a knife and turn out onto a wire rack to cool completely. When cold, dust the top evenly with cocoa and decorate with the gold dragées and geranium petals.

The cake improves with keeping—store in an airtight container for up to 4 days, without decoration.

A pretty and truly scrumptious, tender cake that benefits from using the best white chocolate you can find. Check on the wrapper that it contains only cocoa butter, sugar, and milk solids and no other fat—this way you will get the best flavor. If you are pushed for time, dry the rose petals out in an oven set to the very lowest convection setting and leave the oven door slightly ajar.

WHITE CHOCOLATE MASCARPONE CAKE

3–4 tablespoons raspberry liqueur or raspberry vodka (optional)

CRYSTALLIZED ROSE PETALS

1 egg white

petals of 2 white or cream roses, rinsed and dried

superfine sugar, to sprinkle

CAKE BATTER

3½ oz white chocolate (over 25% cocoa butter)

1½ sticks (12 tablespoons) unsalted butter, softened

1 cup granulated sugar

3 large eggs, separated, at room temperature

1 teaspoon pure vanilla essence

2 cups self-rising flour

6 tablespoons buttermilk or sour cream

CREAMY WHITE CHOCOLATE ICING

6 oz white chocolate (over 25% cocoa butter)

12 oz mascarpone or soft cream cheese, at room temperature

3½ tablespoons unsalted butter, at room temperature

1 teaspoon pure vanilla essence

about 2 cups confectioners' sugar, sifted

a pastry brush

a 9-inch springform cake pan

SERVES 8

To crystallize the rose petals, beat the egg white until loosely frothy, then paint onto the rose petals with a pastry brush. Sprinkle with sugar to coat completely, arrange on a wire rack or waxed paper and leave in a warm place to dry out and crisp—at least overnight. Let cool, then store between layers of paper towels in an airtight container.

Preheat the oven to 350°F. Grease the bottom and sides of the springform pan and baseline with nonstick parchment paper. Dust the sides with flour and tap out the excess.

To make the cake batter, melt the chocolate with 6 tablespoons water according to the instructions on page 17. Using an electric mixer, cream the butter and sugar in a large bowl for about 5 minutes until pale and fluffy. Gradually beat in the egg yolks, one at a time, then beat in the melted white chocolate and the vanilla essence. Using a large metal spoon, fold in half of the flour, then the buttermilk, and then the remaining flour. Using the electric mixer with clean beaters, beat the egg whites in a clean, dry bowl until just stiff but not dry. Beat one-third of the beaten egg whites into the cake mixture to loosen it, then carefully fold in the rest.

Spoon the batter into the prepared springform pan. Bake for 35–40 minutes, or until the cake springs back when touched in the center and a fine skewer inserted in the center comes out clean. Remove from the oven and let cool for 10 minutes in the pan, then turn out onto a wire rack, peel off the lining paper, and let cool completely.

To make the creamy white chocolate icing, melt the chocolate according to the instructions on page 17 and leave until almost cold. With an electric mixer, beat in the mascarpone, butter, and vanilla essence until smooth. Beat in the confectioners' sugar until creamy and spreadable—you may not need it all. Cover and keep at room temperature.

Place the cake on a serving platter and prick all over with a skewer. Spoon over the raspberry liqueur and let soak in for 30 minutes. Spread the icing all over the cake. Refrigerate until needed and scatter with the rose petals just before serving.

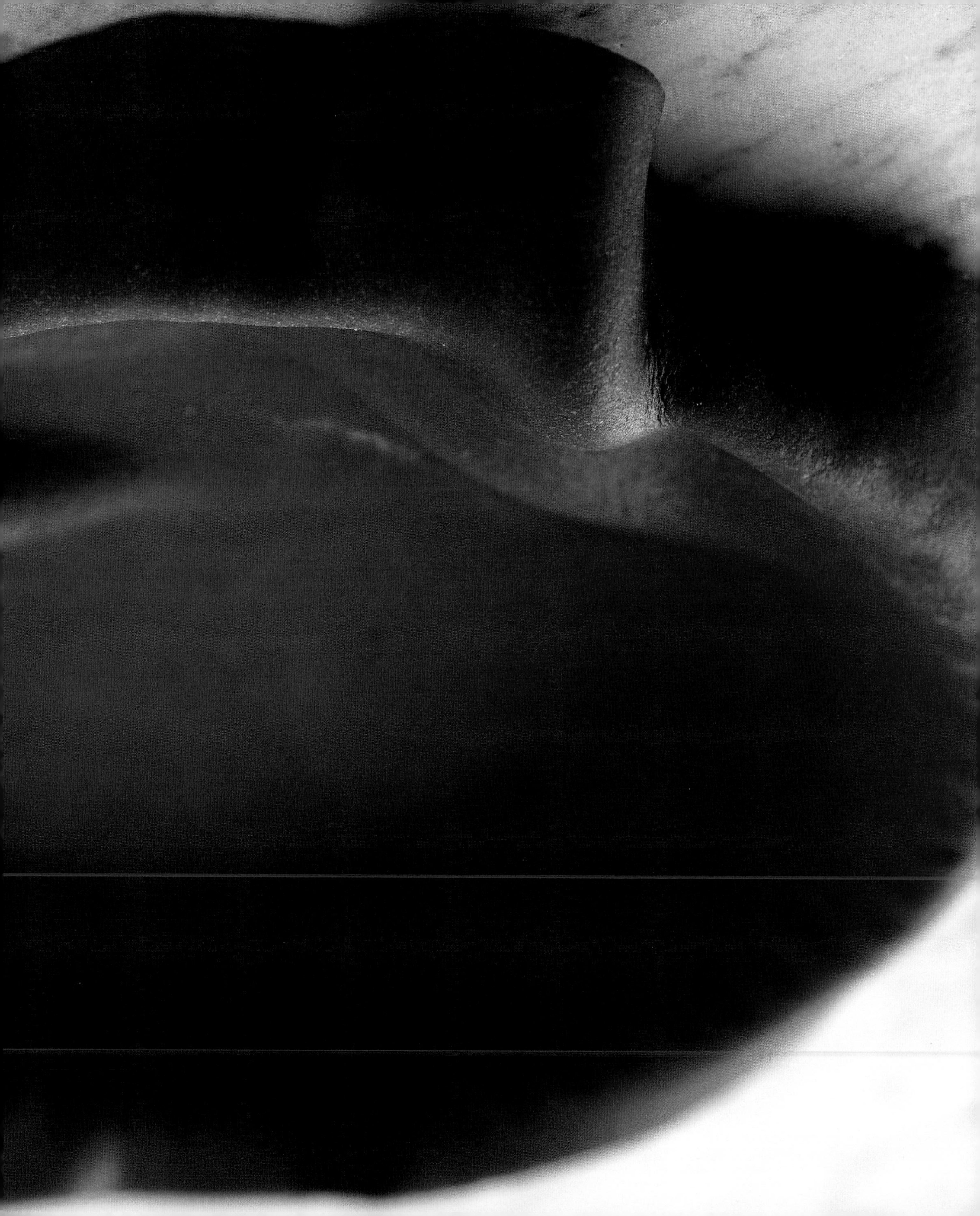

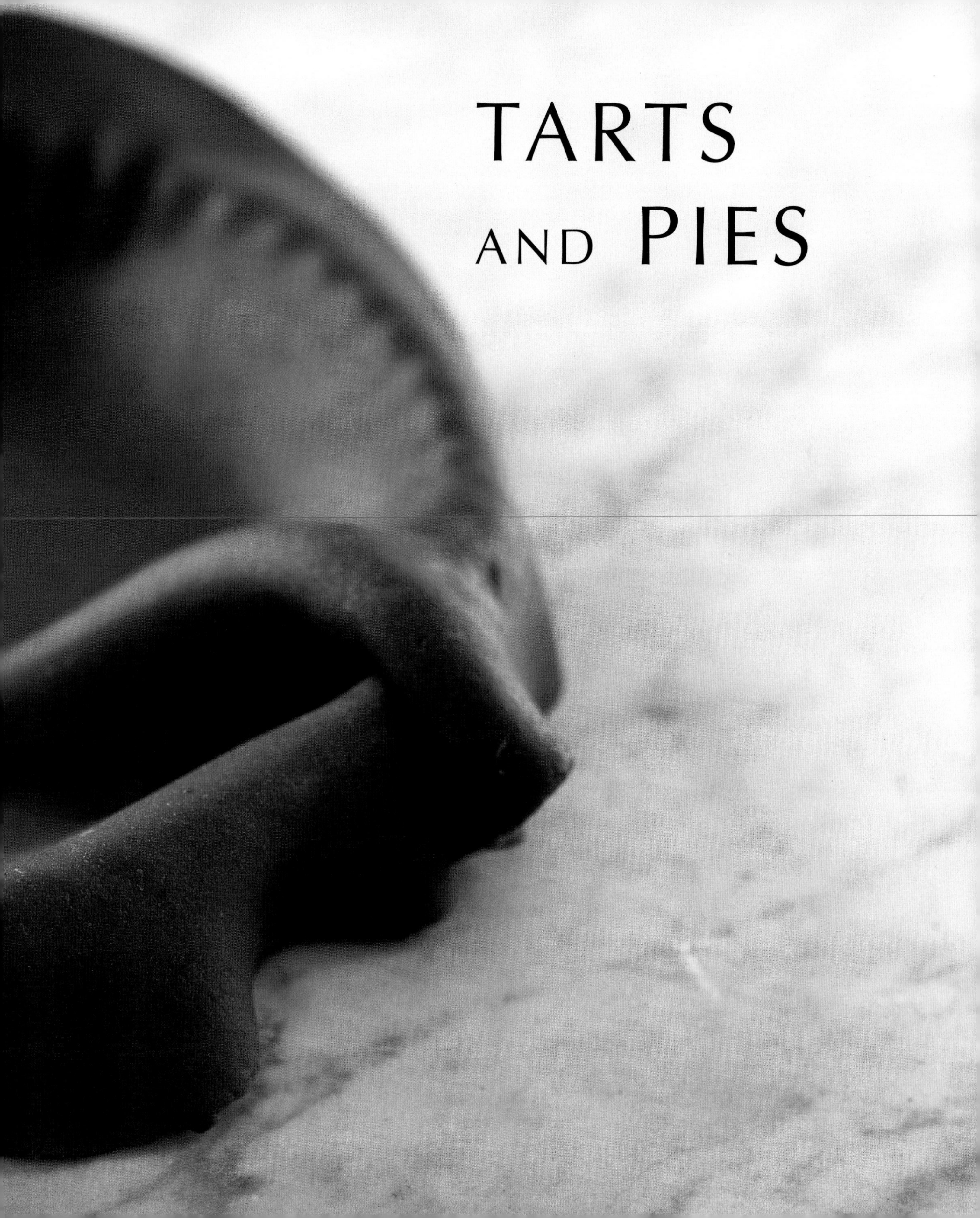

TARTS AND PIES

This is wickedly delicious. Use the darkest chocolate you can find and serve in thin slices. The higher the percentage of cocoa solids in the chocolate, the more intense this is. Use a high-quality chocolate like Amedei Tuscan Black and you won't be disappointed. The filling is gooey and rich and needs nothing more than a dollop of crème fraîche or some fresh cream served with it. I like to add a touch of magic with some edible silver leaf known as varak *in India, which is said to have an aphrodisiac effect. The pastry crust is essentially the classic French sweet pastry, but with a chocolatey twist. It can burn very easily due to the high sugar content, so watch it like a hawk when it is in the oven—time it! This is used for all types of French* pâtisserie *and tartlets as it holds its shape well when baking and is quite robust when filled.*

BLACK MAGIC TART

edible silver leaf, to decorate
confectioners' sugar, to dust
crème fraîche, to serve

CHOCOLATE PATE SUCREE

1 cup plus 2 tablespoons all-purpose flour
5 tablespoons unsweetened cocoa
a pinch of salt
½ cup confectioners' sugar
5 tablespoons unsalted butter, cubed, at room temperature
2 egg yolks
½ teaspoon pure vanilla essence or chocolate extract (see page 31)
2–3 tablespoons chilled water

FILLING

14 oz dark chocolate (60–70% cocoa solids)
1 stick (8 tablespoons) unsalted butter, cubed
5 large eggs, separated
½ cup plus 2 tablespoons granulated sugar
⅔ cup heavy cream, at room temperature
3 tablespoons dark rum or chocolate liqueur

a 10-inch springform tart pan, 1¼ inches deep, with a removable base
baking beans
a pastry brush

SERVES 8

To make the chocolate pâte sucrée, sift the flour, cocoa, and salt onto a sheet of waxed paper.

Put the sugar, butter, egg yolks, and vanilla essence in a food processor and process until smooth. Add the water and process again. Pour in the dry ingredients and work until just combined. Turn out onto a lightly floured work surface and knead gently until smooth. Form into a disk and wrap in plastic wrap. Refrigerate for at least 30 minutes.

Remove the pastry from the fridge and bring to room temperature before rolling out. Preheat the oven to 375°F.

Roll the pastry out thinly on a lightly floured work surface—this is quite a delicate pastry to roll so be sure to use enough (but not too much) flour. Use to line the tart pan. Prick the pastry all over with a fork, then refrigerate or freeze for 15 minutes.

Line the pastry crust with aluminum foil or parchment paper, fill with baking beans, and bake blind for 15 minutes. Remove the foil and beans, reduce the oven temperature to 350°F, and return to the oven for 10–15 minutes to dry out and brown—watch it very carefully because it can burn easily. Remove from the oven. Leave the oven on.

To make the filling, melt the chocolate with the butter according to the instructions on page 17. Remove the bowl from the heat and let cool for about 1 minute.

Put the egg yolks and sugar in a bowl and beat with an electric mixer until pale and creamy. Stir the cream and rum into the melted chocolate mixture, then quickly fold in the egg yolk mixture. Whisk the egg whites in a clean, dry bowl until soft peaks form. Quickly fold into the chocolate mixture with a metal spoon.

Pour the filling into the pastry crust and bake for 20–25 minutes until puffed and a bit wobbly in the center. Remove from the oven and let cool—the filling will sink and firm up as it cools. Decorate by delicately applying silver leaf to the top of the tart with a pastry brush, then dust with confectioners' sugar and serve at room temperature with a dollop of crème fraîche.

Everyone in Italy knows this fabulous cake filled with chocolate custard cream and topped with crunchy pine nuts. The fragrance of this cake is so evocative that when I bake this in Italy, people seem to crawl out of the woodwork, sniffing the air and asking if there's a Torta del Nonno *in the oven.*

TORTA DEL NONNO (GRANDFATHER'S CAKE)

2 egg yolks, beaten, to glaze
4–6 tablespoons pine nuts
confectioners' sugar, to dust

PASTRY

1½ sticks (12 tablespoons) unsalted butter, softened
½ cup granulated sugar
2 egg yolks
finely grated peel of 1 unwaxed orange
1 teaspoon pure vanilla essence
a pinch of salt
2 cups all-purpose flour

CHOCOLATE CUSTARD FILLING

2¼ cups milk
1½ oz dark chocolate (60–70% cocoa solids), finely chopped
2 egg yolks
⅓ cup granulated sugar
1 tablespoon flour, cornstarch, or potato starch
3 tablespoons unsweetened cocoa
½ teaspoon pure vanilla essence

a 9-inch tart pan
baking beans
a pastry brush

SERVES 8

To make the pastry, cream the butter and sugar in a large bowl, using an electric mixer, until light and fluffy. Beat in the egg yolks, orange peel, vanilla essence, and salt. Stir in the flour until almost mixed. Transfer to a lightly floured work surface and knead gently until smooth. Divide into two pieces—one slightly bigger than the other. Form into disks, wrap in plastic wrap, and refrigerate for at least 30 minutes.

Roll out the larger piece of pastry as thinly as possible and use to line the tart pan. Prick the pastry all over with a fork and freeze for at least 15 minutes.

Preheat the oven to 375°F. Line the tart with aluminum foil or parchment paper, fill with baking beans, and bake blind for 15 minutes. Remove the foil and baking beans and return to the oven for a further 10 minutes to dry out. Remove from the oven and let cool. (Leave the oven on.)

Meanwhile, to make the chocolate custard filling, heat the milk with the chocolate in a large pan. When it is just about to boil, take it off the heat. Beat the egg yolks with the sugar in a large bowl, then beat in the flour and cocoa. Beat in the hot chocolate milk. Return the mixture to the pan and heat gently, stirring until starting to thicken. Once it reaches a very slow boil, simmer for 2 minutes, then stir in the vanilla essence. Pour into the cooled pastry crust and let cool.

Roll the remaining pastry out to a circle that is slightly larger than the diameter of the tart pan. Brush the rim of the pastry crust with the beaten egg yolks and cover the filling with the pastry circle, pressing it firmly against the cooked edges, then trim away the excess. Brush the pastry with more egg yolk and scatter over the pine nuts. Make a couple of air holes in the top. Bake for 1 hour, then remove from the oven and let cool completely. Dust with confectioners' sugar and serve.

This is my variation on the classic Normandy apple and almond tart. Frangipane is the term for an almond-flavored cream, and in my version here, it has become a soft, chocolatey almond sponge. Pears, chocolate, and almonds go so well with each other, especially if you choose pears that are not too ripe and still slightly firm. The ground almonds keep the rich, buttery filling moist. Don't forget to add the chocolate liqueur—it makes this tart truly special.

PEAR AND CHOCOLATE FRANGIPANE TART

4 medium, firm pears, unpeeled

⅔ cup seedless raspberry jam

2 tablespoons Ruby Port

toasted shredded or slivered almonds, to scatter (optional)

light cream, to serve (optional)

PASTRY

2 cups all-purpose flour

1 teaspoon salt

1 stick (8 tablespoons) unsalted butter, softened

1 large egg yolk

2½–3 tablespoons chilled water

CHOCOLATE FRANGIPANE FILLING

6½ tablespoons unsalted butter, softened

½ cup granulated sugar

2 eggs, beaten

1–2 tablespoons chocolate liqueur

⅔ cup ground almonds

2 tablespoons unsweetened cocoa

a shallow 10-inch tart pan

a pastry brush

SERVES 8–10

To make the pastry, sift the flour and salt onto a sheet of waxed paper. Put the butter and egg yolk in a food processor and blend until smooth. Add the chilled water and blend again. Pour in the dry ingredients and blend until just combined. Turn out onto a lightly floured work surface and knead gently until smooth. Form into a disk, wrap in plastic wrap, and refrigerate for at least 30 minutes. Bring to room temperature before rolling out.

To make the chocolate frangipane filling, put the butter in a large bowl and beat with an electric mixer until creamy. Gradually add the sugar and beat until pale and fluffy. Gradually beat in the eggs and the chocolate liqueur, then stir in the ground almonds and the cocoa. Cover and set aside.

Roll out the pastry on a lightly floured work surface and use to line the tart pan. Prick the pastry all over with a fork and refrigerate until firm.

Preheat the oven to 400°F, and put a heavy baking sheet on the middle shelf.

Spread the chocolate frangipane evenly over the chilled pastry crust.

Halve the pears and scoop out the cores. Cut each half into thirds and arrange them randomly over the chocolate frangipane.

Transfer the tart to the preheated baking sheet and bake for 10–15 minutes, or until the pastry starts to brown. Reduce the oven temperature to 350°F and bake for a further 15–20 minutes or until the pears are tender and the frangipane is set. Remove from the oven and transfer to a wire rack to cool.

About 20 minutes before serving, melt the jam with the port in a small pan and boil for 1 minute to make a glaze. Remove the tart from the pan, brush with the glaze, scatter with the almonds, if using, and serve at room temperature—never chilled—with cream, if using.

What could be more heavenly than a melting, flaky chocolate crust hiding a rich, soft, moist chocolate and almond filling? The ultimate would be made with buttery homemade puff pastry dough, but if you buy it ready-made, it will save hours! You can leave out the Chocolate Crème Pâtissière if you like—the result will be denser but just as delicious. Always serve this warm, not hot, with fresh cream or Crème Anglaise.

CHOCOLATE ALMOND PITHIVIERS

20 oz puff pastry dough, thawed if frozen

1 egg yolk, lightly beaten with 1 tablespoon milk, to glaze

3 tablespoons confectioners' sugar

half-and-half or Crème Anglaise (page 137), to serve (optional)

CHOCOLATE ALMOND CREAM

¼ cup Chocolate Crème Pâtissière (page 137)

4 tablespoons unsalted butter, at room temperature

½ cup less 1 tablespoon sugar, sifted

1 large egg

scant ½ cup ground almonds

2 tablespoons unsweetened cocoa

2 tablespoons chocolate liqueur (optional)

1½ oz dark chocolate (60–70% cocoa solids), grated

an 8-inch plate or flan ring

a 9½-inch plate or flan ring

a pastry brush

SERVES 8

To make the chocolate almond cream, cream the butter and confectioners' sugar together with an electric mixer in a medium bowl until pale and fluffy. Gradually beat in the egg, then the ground almonds, cocoa, and liqueur, if using. Finally, beat in the Chocolate Crème Pâtissière and the grated chocolate. Set aside.

Divide the puff pastry dough in two—one slightly bigger than the other (about 12 oz and 8 oz). To make the base, roll out the smaller piece of pastry directly onto a lightly floured baking sheet, into a rough circle about 10¼ inches in diameter and ⅛ inch thick. To make the top, roll out the bigger piece of pastry to a circle of the same diameter, but about 3/16 inch thick.

Gently press the 8-inch plate or flan ring onto the pastry base, centering it carefully. It should make a light but visible indentation. Spoon the chocolate almond cream into the center of the pastry base, then spread it evenly within the marked circle. Glaze the exposed pastry edge with some egg-milk wash.

Place the second circle of pastry on top and press around the dome of the chocolate almond cream first to seal it in, then press around the pastry edge. Set the 9½-inch plate or flan ring centrally over the pastry and cut all the way around it to make a perfect circle. Discard the excess pastry. Refrigerate the pie for 30 minutes.

Preheat the oven to 475°F, if possible, or its hottest setting.

Remove the pie from the fridge and, using a small sharp knife, cut the outer rim into a scallop-shaped border. Glaze the entire surface of the pie with egg-milk wash, then, with the point of a knife, score faint curved lines spiraling from the center of the cake to the edge, like sunrays.

Bake for 10 minutes to set the pastry, then reduce the oven temperature to 400°F and bake for a further 25 minutes. Increase the oven temperature to 425°F. Remove the pie from the oven and sift the confectioners' sugar evenly over the surface. Bake for a further 5 minutes. Serve warm, with half-and-half if you like.

Note: You can freeze the pie, unbaked, for up to 1 week. To bake from frozen, leave at room temperature for 30 minutes, then bake while still semi-frozen, allowing an extra 10 minutes in the oven at the 400°F stage.

A gorgeous fudgy, nutty tart made all the more delicious by the addition of bourbon. Instead of pecans, you can use a mixture of your favorite nuts, although creamier nuts, such as walnuts, brazils, and macadamias are best. Making your own pastry for this will make all the difference—there's nothing to beat a light, crumbly, buttery pastry crust. Freeze any leftover pastry to make tartlets—or make little individual tartlets instead for afternoon tea! You can also make this with Chocolate Pâte Sucrée (page 63).

CHOCOLATE, BOURBON, AND PECAN TART WITH COFFEE BEAN SAUCE

1 recipe Coffee Bean Sauce, flavored with bourbon (page 137)

RICH SHORT CRUST PASTRY

1⅔ cups all-purpose flour

6 tablespoons unsweetened cocoa

2 tablespoons confectioners' sugar

½ teaspoon salt

1 stick (8 tablespoons) unsalted butter, cubed

2 egg yolks mixed with 2 tablespoons ice water

1 egg, beaten, to glaze

CHOCOLATE NUT FILLING

4 oz dark chocolate (60–70% cocoa solids)

3 tablespoons unsalted butter, cubed

3 large eggs, beaten

⅔ cup pure maple syrup

3 tablespoons bourbon

1⅔ cups pecan nuts

a 9-inch tart pan
baking beans

SERVES 6

To make the rich short crust pastry, sift the flour, cocoa, confectioners' sugar, and salt in the bowl of a food processor. Add the butter and process for about 30 seconds until the mixture resembles very fine bread crumbs. Pour in the egg yolks and ice water and pulse for 10 seconds. The dough should start to come together in large, raggy lumps. If not, add another tablespoon of ice water and pulse again. As soon as the dough forms one big lump (don't overprocess or the pastry will be tough), tip out onto a lightly floured work surface and knead lightly into a firm but malleable dough. Shape into a disk, wrap in plastic wrap, and refrigerate for at least 30 minutes.

Remove the pastry from the fridge and bring to room temperature. Preheat the oven to 375°F.

Roll the pastry out on a lightly floured work surface and use to line the tart pan. Prick the pastry all over with a fork and refrigerate or freeze for 15 minutes. Line the pastry crust with aluminum foil or parchment paper, fill with baking beans, and bake blind for 10–12 minutes. Glaze the pastry crust with the beaten egg and bake for a further 5–10 minutes. Remove from the oven and let cool.

To make the chocolate nut filling, reduce the oven temperature to 325°F. Melt the chocolate with the butter according to the instructions on page 17. Put the eggs, maple syrup, and bourbon in a bowl and beat well. Add to the melted chocolate (still in a bowl over a pan of simmering water). Stir well, and keep stirring over low heat until the mixture starts to thicken. Stir in the pecan nuts and pour into the pastry crust.

Bake for 35–40 minutes, or until just set—the filling will still be a bit wobbly.

Serve the tart warm with the Coffee Bean Sauce.

THE DUTCH AND COCOA

For more than a century after its discovery, the Spanish had the monopoly on cocoa and kept the drink a coveted secret. In 1585, Dutch pirates encountered the precious bean cargo when they plundered a Spanish ship and threw it overboard thinking it was sheep's droppings! Little did they know that the Netherlands would become the world's largest exporter of cocoa products in the twenty-first century.

By the end of the seventeenth century, due to the universal popularity of the hot drink, the Dutch East India Company was growing cacao in the new colony of Surinam (formerly a British colony) and shipping it to be ground in Amsterdam. The trade grew and grew and by the end of the eighteenth century, there were more than 30 chocolate (the drink) factories in Amsterdam. The demand for chocolate was so high that mustard mills were converted into chocolate mills. Chocolate houses were outnumbering coffee houses.

The Dutch chocolate revolution didn't end there. A Dutch doctor, Conraad van Houten, developed a method of pressing, whereby the drink could be greatly improved. Until now, the problem with the hot chocolate drink was that there was always a layer of greasy cocoa butter and scum floating on top. Various methods had been used to absorb the naturally occurring fat. On both sides of the Channel, ground cocoa was experimentally mixed with ground acorns, potato starch, arrowroot, and even powdered seashells to make it more palatable. Powdered brick dust, lead-based pigments, and rust were added for color, and analysis commissioned by *The Lancet* in 1851 showed that 90% of brands tested were not pure crushed cacao bean.

In 1828, van Houten came up with two innovations to refine the quality of drinking chocolate and cocoa. Aided by the invention of powerful hydraulic presses in the Industrial Revolution, he patented a method of pressing most of the cocoa butter out of the cocoa liquor to make a cocoa presscake. This was finely ground into almost fat-free cocoa powder, producing a valuable by-product—cocoa butter. He also developed a method to enhance the taste and color of cacao during the production process through alkalization (the addition of a solution of alkali salt, normally potassium carbonate). This process became known as Dutching (see page 11), and made the cacao less bitter, neutralizing the natural acidity of the bean. Dutched cocoa became milder in taste, with a warmer reddish tint, and when mixed with hot water, it made an infinitely superior drink to its rustic, gritty predecessor.

Today, un-Dutched powdered cocoa is generally described as "natural" or "pure," is a much lighter color, slightly acidic (with a stronger chocolate flavor), and generally not used to make chocolate. I use natural cocoa in recipes which include baking soda (an alkali), since combining the two creates a natural rising action that allows the mixture to rise and lighten during baking. I use milder, darker Dutched cocoa for coating truffles and sifting over cakes. The fat content of the cocoa can also affect its color and is normally between 20–22% (although it is possible to find 15–17% and 10–12%). Fat-free cocoa is not legally called cocoa powder and is mixed with fat, sugar, and other ingredients to produce chocolate-flavored coverings, cake mixes, and drinks.

The unique taste and aroma of cocoa is used in many food products to enhance flavor and color, but it is best-known today for making chocolate.

It is not only the type of bean and the drying process that determine the color and the taste, but also the manufacturing process (see page 12 for the complete process). It is at the grinding stage that powdered cocoa is obtained. Most cocoa manufacturers can customize their cocoa for individual bulk customers according to their needs, and a variety of colors can be produced by carefully adjusting the pH levels, the moisture content, and roasting temperatures and times.

Today, the Netherlands is the world's market leader for cocoa with a share of about 25%. Major outlets are Germany, the USA, France, Italy, and Belgium. The Netherlands and France are the most important producers of cocoa butter in Europe, the top buyers being Germany, Belgium, France, the UK, and Switzerland. The Netherlands processes 450,000 tons of cacao beans, making it the most important processor in the world. Other major European players are Germany, the UK, and France. The average per capita consumption of chocolate in the Netherlands is 11 lb per year.

Right: powdered cocoa varies in color depending on its fat content and whether it has been Dutched

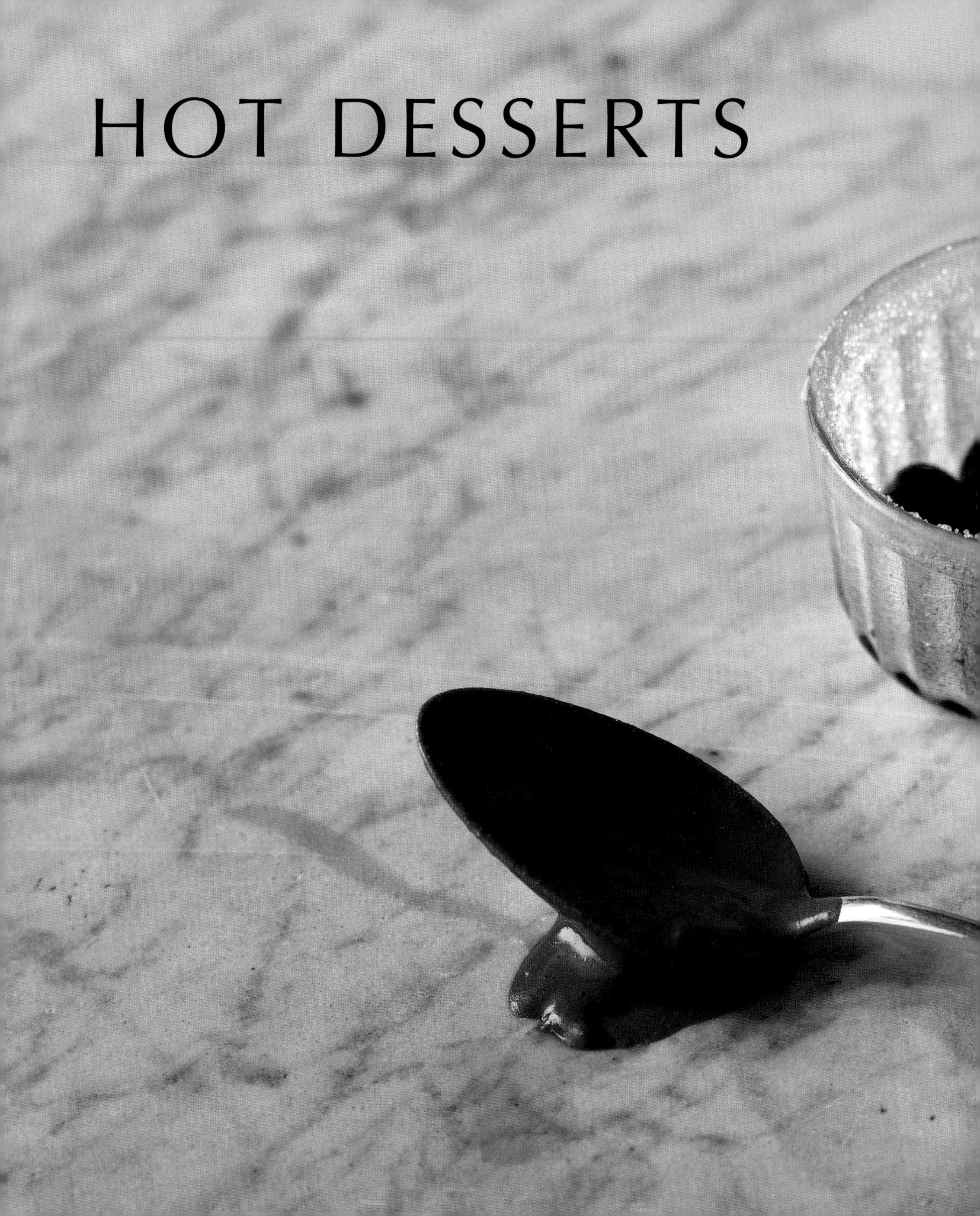

HOT DESSERTS

There is nothing better on a cold winter's day than the sound (and smell) of a steamed pudding gently rattling in its pan, waiting to be turned out and smothered in Chocolate Crème Anglaise. This pudding looks good enough to serve at a dinner party, the orange slices glowing out from the dark, sticky base. Smaller oranges are best here, and don't peel them—they are cooked with their skins for maximum effect. The dates keep the dessert beautifully moist.

CHOCOLATE, ORANGE, AND DATE STEAMED PUDDING

Chocolate Crème Anglaise (page 137), to serve

½ cup sugar

2–3 seedless oranges

14 tablespoons unsalted butter, softened

1 cup dark brown sugar

finely grated peel of 1 unwaxed orange

3 tablespoons fine-cut orange marmalade

3 eggs, beaten

1 tablespoon orange-flower water (optional)

1 cup plus 2 tablespoons all-purpose flour

6 tablespoons unsweetened cocoa

2 teaspoons baking powder

¾ cup pitted dates, chopped

a 6-cup pudding basin (deep heatproof bowl)

SERVES 6–8

First make a sugar syrup. Pour ⅔ cup water into a small saucepan and add the sugar. Cook over gentle heat until dissolved.

Slice each orange thinly into about 6 neat slices. Submerge them in the sugar syrup. Set a disk of nonstick parchment paper on top and simmer gently for 30–40 minutes. Lift the oranges out with a slotted spoon and drain on a wire rack. Boil the syrup hard until reduced by half and set aside.

Butter the pudding basin and line the base with a small disk of nonstick parchment paper. Place the best orange slice on top of the disk, and use the rest of the slices to line the sides of the basin.

In a large bowl, cream the butter, brown sugar, and orange peel using an electric mixer, until light and fluffy. Beat in the marmalade, then gradually beat in the eggs and orange-flower water, if using, mixing very well between each addition. Sift the flour, cocoa, and baking powder onto a sheet of waxed paper, then fold into the egg mixture. Finally, fold in the dates.

Carefully spoon the pudding mixture into the orange-lined basin. It should come about three-quarters of the way up the sides. Smooth the surface and cover with a disk of nonstick parchment paper. Take a large sheet of aluminum foil and fold it in half. Make a pleat in the center and place over the basin, with the pleat in the center. Press the foil over the side of the basin, tie around the top with kitchen twine and trim away any excess foil. The pleat will open out and allow the pudding to expand during cooking. Stand the basin on a trivet in a large, deep pan and add enough water to come at least 2 inches up the sides. Cover the pan with a lid and simmer gently for 2 hours, topping up the water level from time to time.

Remove the foil and paper disk and insert a small skewer into the center of the pudding. It should come out clean. If not, re-cover and steam for a little longer. Loosen the pudding around the sides with a thin-bladed knife, turn out onto a warm serving dish, and brush with a little of the reserved syrup. Serve with Chocolate Crème Anglaise.

This is truly outrageous, and all the better for it! It's the most decadent version of classic bread and butter pudding I know, and it is equally at home both as an informal indulgence and as a real dinner party treat. Try using the best pains au chocolat *you can find, preferably the ones with twin chocolate bars inside. This recipe will even transform the soft supermarket variety into something sublime!*

PAIN AU CHOCOLAT PUDDING

4 large *pains au chocolat* (preferably with twin chocolate bars in each)

1¼ cups milk

1¼ cups heavy cream

1 vanilla bean, split lengthwise

4 egg yolks

½ cup plus 2 tablespoons granulated sugar

3½ oz dark chocolate (60–70% cocoa solids), grated (or even chocolate chips)

confectioners' sugar, to dust

half-and-half, to serve

a 2-quart shallow baking dish, greased

a large roasting pan

SERVES 6

Cut the *pains au chocolat* into thick slices. Arrange the slices, cut-side up and overlapping, in the prepared baking dish.

Put the milk, cream, and vanilla bean in a pan. Cook over very low heat for about 5 minutes, or until the mixture is almost boiling and well flavored with aromatic vanilla. Remove from the heat.

Preheat the oven to 350°F.

In a large bowl, whisk together the egg yolks and granulated sugar until light and creamy. Strain the flavored milk through a fine strainer into the egg mixture, beating well. Whisk in two-thirds of the grated chocolate. Pour the egg mixture evenly over the *pains au chocolat* and let stand for 10 minutes to allow them to absorb the liquid.

Sprinkle over the remaining chocolate. Put the baking dish in a large roasting pan and pour in enough boiling water to come halfway up the sides of the dish. Bake the pudding for 40–45 minutes, or until the custard is softly set and the top is crisp and golden brown.

Remove from the oven, lift out of the roasting pan, and set aside until just warm. Sprinkle with the confectioners' sugar and serve with half-and-half.

Italian amarena cherries are addictive. Reserve the drained syrup and stir it into the bitter chocolate sauce. All is not lost if the soufflés collapse—just let stand for 5 minutes then turn them out of the ramekins and serve with hot chocolate sauce and whipped cream. I measure my egg whites as a liquid measure for soufflés—it is much more accurate.

BLACK FOREST SOUFFLÉ WITH HOT CHOCOLATE SAUCE

Bitter Chocolate Sauce or White Chocolate Sauce (page 135), to serve

10 oz dark chocolate (60–70% cocoa solids)

⅔ cup drained amarena cherries

4 egg yolks

1 cup egg whites

½ cup superfine sugar

6 large ramekins, greased and dusted with sugar

SERVES 6

Preheat the oven to 425°F.

Melt the chocolate according to the instructions on page 17. Divide the amarena cherries between the ramekins.

Beat the egg yolks into the melted chocolate with a wooden spoon until the mixture becomes thick and stiff.

Using an electric mixer, beat the egg whites in a clean, dry bowl until they form soft peaks. Add the superfine sugar and continue to beat hard for about 3 minutes, or until the whites form soft peaks again and are thick and smooth. Beat a large tablespoon of the meringue into the chocolate mixture, then carefully fold in the remaining meringue with a metal spoon. It is very important at this stage not to overfold and knock out the air, as it is the trapped air in the mixture that makes the soufflés rise.

Divide the mixture between the ramekins and give each one a good tap on the work surface to level the top. Set them on a heavy baking sheet.

Bake for 13–15 minutes, or until they are well risen. Serve immediately with Bitter Chocolate Sauce or White Chocolate Sauce. To eat, dig your spoon into the middle of your soufflé and pour in the sauce. Mmmmmmm!

The pears here absorb the deep, rich flavor of the wine and cinnamon and turn a fabulous color. I like to add fine cornmeal to the cake batter as it gives a lighter texture to the baked cake. Always turn this out while still warm to reveal the pears in all their glorious stickiness.

CHOCOLATE, PORT, AND PEAR UPSIDE-DOWN SPONGE

Crème Anglaise (page 137), to serve
6–8 medium, underripe pears, peeled
1 cinnamon stick
6 tablespoons sugar
⅔ cup Ruby Port
2 cups full-bodied red wine

CAKE BATTER
¾ cup all-purpose flour
3 tablespoons unsweetened cocoa
1 teaspoon baking powder
a pinch of salt
½ cup fine cornmeal
6½ tablespoons unsalted butter, softened
¾ cup plus 2 tablespoons sugar
3 large eggs, separated
1 teaspoon pure vanilla essence
6 tablespoons milk

a 9 x 2-inch heavy round cake pan, greased

SERVES 6

Halve the pears lengthwise and carefully scoop out the core with a teaspoon or melon baller. Put the pears in a wide, shallow sauté pan with the cinnamon and the sugar. Pour over the port and red wine and bring to a boil. Cover and simmer gently for 20 minutes (after which they will still be a little firm). Lift the pears out of the pan with a slotted spoon. Let cool. Boil the reserved wine juices hard until well reduced and syrupy.

Arrange the pears cut-side down around the base of the prepared cake pan (wide ends outward, points toward the middle). Pour over half the wine syrup, reserving the rest. Let cool.

Preheat the oven to 375°F.

To make the cake batter, sift the flour, cocoa, baking powder, and salt in a small bowl and stir in the cornmeal. Using an electric beater, cream the butter and sugar in a large bowl until pale and fluffy, then beat in the egg yolks and vanilla essence. Fold in the flour mixture, then beat in the milk.

Using the electric mixer with clean beaters, beat the egg whites in a clean, dry bowl until they form soft peaks. Using a metal spoon, quickly stir a large spoonful of whites into the cake mixture to loosen it, then gently fold in the remainder. Spoon the cake batter over the pears and smooth the surface.

Bake for 45–60 minutes, or until a metal skewer inserted into the center comes out clean. Remove from the oven and let cool for 10 minutes in the pan. Just before serving, put the pan over low heat for 1 minute to warm the pears and help loosen them from the bottom. Run a knife around the edges to loosen the cake and invert onto a warm serving plate. Brush the pears with the reserved syrup. Serve warm or at room temperature with Crème Anglaise.

Bananas, caramel, and chocolate are just one of the world's best combinations—and this uses a lot of bananas! Cutting them up and standing them upright gives a wonderful deep pie that looks amazing. I tried cooking the chocolate with the caramel, but it tended to burn, so I sprinkled it over the hot tart once it was turned out and the effect was divine. Use nice ripe bananas here. If you want to use fewer bananas, cut them in thick diagonal slices and spread out over the base of the pan in a thinner layer.

BANANA AND CHOCOLATE TARTE TATIN

Bitter Chocolate Sauce (page 135), whipped cream, or Crème Anglaise (page 137), to serve

½ cup sugar

3½ tablespoons unsalted butter

12 medium, ripe bananas

12 oz all-butter puff pastry dough, thawed if frozen

2½ oz dark chocolate (60–70% cocoa solids), finely grated

a flameproof 10-inch cast-iron skillet, heavy cake pan, or Tatin pan

SERVES 8

Preheat the oven to 375°F.

Put the sugar and butter in the cast-iron skillet, heavy cake pan, or Tatin pan. Place over medium heat and cook, stirring every now and then, until the mixture bubbles and turns into a smooth, rich toffee. It will look very grainy to start with and the butter will look as if it has split away from the sugar, but just keep stirring and it will gradually come together. Remove from the heat.

Cut the bananas into 3 even pieces. Arrange them standing upright in the skillet or pan, packing them together.

Roll out the pastry on a lightly floured surface into a rough circle 11 inches across. Lay the pastry over the bananas and tuck the edges down into the skillet to make the rim of the tart. Prick the top of the pastry here and there with a fork, then bake for 35–40 minutes, or until risen and golden. Remove the skillet from the oven and let rest for 10 minutes.

Run a sharp knife around the pastry to free the edges. Pour out any caramel liquid that has gathered in the base and reserve. Invert a serving plate over the top of the skillet. Carefully turn skillet and plate over together, then remove the skillet. Pour over the reserved caramel sauce and immediately sprinkle with the grated chocolate and let melt in the residual heat. Serve cut into wedges with Bitter Chocolate Sauce, whipped cream, or Crème Anglaise.

Rice pudding must be one of my favorite desserts and is made all the more special by the addition of chocolate and boozy, rum-soaked raisins. I like to spoon the warm raisins over the creamy rice pudding, but you could always cook them in the pudding after they have been well and truly steeped in the rum.

CHOCOLATE, RUM, AND RAISIN RICE PUDDING

⅔ cup raisins

⅔ cup dark rum

1 vanilla bean, split lengthwise

1¼ cups milk

1¼ cups evaporated milk

3½ oz dark chocolate (60–70% cocoa solids), chopped or grated

¼ cup short-grain rice

a 1-quart ovenproof dish

SERVES 4

Preheat the oven to 300°F.

Put the raisins and rum in a small pan and bring to a boil. Remove from the heat and transfer to a bowl and cover. Let soak for at least 3 hours or overnight. This can be done days ahead. Store the raisins in a tightly covered jar in the fridge.

Put the vanilla bean, milk, and evaporated milk in a medium pan and bring slowly to a boil. Stir in the chocolate and rice. Stir until the chocolate has melted, then pour into the ovenproof dish. Bake for about 3 hours or until a brown skin forms on top and the rice is cooked and creamy. (Alternatively, if you don't like the skin on traditional rice pudding, simmer very slowly on top of the stove for about 1 hour until thick and creamy.)

To serve, put the soaked raisins and their liquid into a small pan and warm them through. Serve the raisins spooned over the rice pudding.

CHILLED DESSERTS

A semifreddo is an ice cream made with a meringue base, and it will usually hold its shape even after thawing. When frozen, the mixture is soft enough to cut through with a hot knife. This is best made in little molds then turned out and decorated with chocolate. However, I have also made it in a traditional Bûche de Noël ice-cream mold (found in a French antique shop) which I first lined with melted chocolate then filled with semifreddo. It looked wonderful—see the picture on the left. Gianduja *is a chocolate and hazelnut mixture famously from Piemonte in Italy.*

GIANDUJA SEMIFREDDO

4 oz skinned hazelnuts

4 oz dark chocolate (60–70% cocoa solids), plus extra to decorate

2½ cups heavy cream

2 eggs, separated

1¼ cups confectioners' sugar

8 individual ice-cream molds

a freezerproof tray

SERVES 8 GENEROUSLY

Preheat the oven to 375°F.

Put the hazelnuts on a baking sheet and roast in the oven for about 8 minutes, or until golden brown. Remove from the oven and let cool completely, then grind very finely in an electric spice grinder.

Melt the chocolate according to the instructions on page 17. Reserve the pan of warm water off the heat.

Beat the cream until it just holds its shape, then fold in the hazelnuts. In a large bowl, beat the egg yolks with 2 tablespoons of the confectioners' sugar until pale and creamy. Stir the melted chocolate into the egg yolk mixture, then set over the reserved pan of warm water to keep from setting.

Working quickly, beat the egg whites in a clean, dry bowl until they form floppy peaks. Add the remaining confectioners' sugar, a spoonful at a time, beating between each addition, until very thick. Fold the hazelnut cream into the chocolate mixture, then fold in the meringue mixture with a metal spoon.

Spoon the mixture into the molds and smooth the surface. Place a circle of nonstick parchment paper over each one, set on a freezerproof tray, and freeze for about 12 hours. Alternatively, freeze in a larger container to serve in scoops. Transfer to the fridge for 10 minutes to soften before serving.

To serve, dip the molds in a basin of warm water for 10 seconds, then, if the molds are plastic, give a gentle squeeze and the semifreddos should pop out. If the molds are metal, slip a thin-bladed knife down one side to loosen. Invert onto chilled plates. To decorate, melt some dark chocolate and pipe it in swirling filigree patterns over waxed paper. Refrigerate for a couple of minutes, then break the filigree into pieces and use to decorate the semifreddo. Alternatively, decorate with chocolate shavings, curls, or thin squares of chocolate.

Variation: Brush the inside of a metal ice-cream mold with melted chocolate, making sure it's not too thick. Refrigerate until set. Spoon the cold semifreddo mixture into the mold and smooth the surface. Cover with nonstick parchment paper and freeze for at least 12 hours. Place a plate on the base of the mold, turn upside down, and give a sharp tap on the work surface—the chocolate shrinks as it freezes and the whole thing will pop out.

What a combination—the sorbet is rich, soft, smooth, and dark and the ice cream is velvety and voluptuous with the occasional crunch of macadamia nuts. This is a dreamy, creamy ice cream which relies entirely on using the best-quality white chocolate you can buy, otherwise the flavor will suffer. It is the cocoa butter in the white chocolate that gives it a mild chocolate taste, so make sure it contains more than 25% cocoa butter.

CHOCOLATE SORBET WITH WHITE CHOCOLATE AND MACADAMIA NUT ICE CREAM

CHOCOLATE SORBET

1¼ cups granulated sugar

½ cup premium unsweetened cocoa, sifted

2½ oz dark chocolate (60–70% cocoa solids), grated

2 teaspoons pure vanilla essence

1 teaspoon instant espresso coffee powder

MAKES ABOUT 1 QUART

WHITE CHOCOLATE AND MACADAMIA NUT ICE CREAM

3 cups heavy cream

1 cup whole milk (or evaporated milk)

6 oz premium white chocolate (over 25% cocoa butter), chopped

4 egg yolks

¾ cup granulated sugar

1 cup macadamia nuts, roughly chopped, plus extra to serve

MAKES ABOUT 1¼ QUARTS

an ice-cream maker (optional)

a freezerproof tray or container

stemmed glasses, chilled

To make the chocolate sorbet, put 2 cups water, the sugar, and cocoa in a pan and beat well to combine. Bring slowly to a boil, stirring until the sugar has dissolved. Boil fast for 5 minutes to make a thin chocolate syrup. Remove from the heat, add the grated chocolate, vanilla essence, and espresso powder, and stir until melted. Let cool, then refrigerate.

If using an ice-cream maker, churn-freeze the chilled mixture in two batches. This will take 20–30 minutes. It will increase in volume as it thickens and freezes. Stop churning when thick and smooth, then transfer to a chilled freezerproof tray, cover, and freeze. If you don't have an ice-cream maker, put the mixture in a freezerproof tray or container and freeze until it is frozen around the edges. Mash well with a fork and return to the freezer. Continue mashing with a fork and freezing the mixture until thick and smooth, about 2 hours. Transfer to the fridge to soften for 10–15 minutes before serving. The sorbet will be quite soft when fully frozen due to the high quantity of sugar.

To make the white chocolate and macadamia nut ice cream, put the cream and milk in a pan and bring to a boil. Add the chocolate and stir until melted.

Using an electric mixer, beat the egg yolks and sugar together until pale and fluffy. Pour the chocolate milk onto the egg mixture, stirring all the time until well blended. Return to the pan and cook over gentle heat for 5 minutes, or until slightly thickened—do not allow to get too hot or it will curdle. Remove from the heat and let cool, stirring from time to time until cold.

Churn-freeze in an ice-cream maker or put in the freezer, as above. When smooth and thick, stir in the macadamia nuts. Transfer to the fridge to soften for 20 minutes before serving.

To serve, put a scoop of sorbet, then a scoop of ice cream in each glass and scatter with chopped macadamia nuts.

My sister Jacks is crazy about the Alps and anything alpine, and found a cake pan in Paris that looks like a mountain range. That was my inspiration here—to make an ice cream to suit an alpine mold. What could be more perfect than an ice cream that tastes of smooth, creamy Swiss milk chocolate studded with white nougat, resembling a triangular Swiss chocolate bar? This truly is a gorgeous ice cream with a satin-like texture interrupted by melting honeyed, nutty nougat. One scoop is not enough. Serve with white chocolate sauce to resemble snowy slopes. Kids go mad for this!

SWISS MOUNTAIN ICE CREAM

White Chocolate Sauce (page 135)
2 cups whole milk
1 cup sweetened condensed milk
¾ cup granulated sugar
2 tablespoons unsweetened cocoa
14 oz premium milk chocolate (over 32% cocoa solids), chopped
1 teaspoon pure vanilla essence
1½ cups whipping or heavy cream, chilled
6½ oz white nougat, roughly chopped

an ice-cream maker (optional)
a freezerproof tray or container
a mountain-shaped mold (optional)

MAKES ABOUT 2 QUARTS

Put the milk, condensed milk, sugar, and cocoa in a pan, bring to a boil, then simmer gently for 5 minutes, stirring constantly. Stir in the chocolate and let melt, stirring occasionally. Let cool completely, then add the vanilla essence and refrigerate for about 1 hour.

Stir the cream into the mixture, then churn-freeze in an ice-cream maker in two batches. This will take 20–30 minutes. It will increase in volume as it thickens and freezes. Stop churning when thick and smooth, add the nougat, and churn to mix, then transfer to a chilled freezerproof tray, cover, and freeze. If you don't have an ice-cream maker, put the mixture in a freezerproof tray or container and freeze until it is frozen around the edges. Mash well with a fork and return to the freezer. Continue mashing with a fork and freezing the mixture until thick and smooth, about 2 hours. Stir in the nougat. At this stage you can pack it into a mold and return to the freezer.

If the ice cream is in a mold, remove from the freezer and dip briefly in hot water to melt the outside. Invert onto a chilled plate, lifting off the mold. If the ice cream is in a container, transfer to the fridge to soften for 20 minutes before serving in scoops. Drizzle with hot White Chocolate Sauce and serve.

This is just about the richest, most luscious ice cream you will ever taste, conjuring up childhood memories of a refreshing chocolate malt on a hot summer's day. Topped with a hot fudge sauce, this ice cream shoots off the superlative scale. Don't use your very best dark chocolate for this—it will be wasted.

CHOCOLATE MALTED ICE CREAM WITH RICH CHOCOLATE SAUCE

Rich Chocolate Fudge Sauce (page 135)

1¼ cups heavy cream

1¼ cups milk

⅔ cup chocolate-flavored instant malted milk powder (such as Ovaltine)

2½ oz dark chocolate (60–70% cocoa solids), grated

6 egg yolks

¾ cup plus 2 tablespoons sugar

2–3 tablespoons chocolate liqueur (optional)

an ice-cream maker (optional)

a freezerproof tray or container

SERVES 6–8 (MAKES 1 QUART)

Put the cream and milk in a pan and bring to a boil. Remove from the heat and beat in the malted milk powder. Add the chocolate and stir until melted.

Using an electric mixer, beat the egg yolks and sugar together until pale and fluffy. Pour in the malt mixture, stirring all the time until well blended. Return to the pan and cook for 5 minutes, or until slightly thickened—do not allow to get too hot or it will curdle. Remove the pan from the heat and let cool, stirring from time to time until cold. Add the liqueur, if using.

If using an ice-cream maker, churn-freeze the mixture in two batches. This will take 20–30 minutes. It will increase in volume as it thickens and freezes. Stop churning when thick and smooth, then transfer to a chilled freezerproof tray, cover, and freeze. If you don't have an ice-cream maker, put the mixture in a freezerproof tray or container and freeze until it is frozen around the edges. Mash well with a fork and return to the freezer. Continue mashing with a fork and freezing the mixture until thick and smooth, about 2 hours. Transfer to the fridge to soften for 20 minutes before serving.

Serve in generous scoops, drizzled with Rich Chocolate Fudge Sauce.

Reserve your best white, milk, and dark chocolates for this dessert. The custards are silky smooth when baked to perfection—don't rush them or raise the temperature otherwise the consistency will be ruined. For an even richer custard, use heavy cream instead of the milk-cream combination.

THREE LITTLE CHOCOLATE POTS

1⅓ cups milk

1⅓ cups light cream

2 tablespoons sugar

4 large egg yolks

2 whole eggs

1 teaspoon pure vanilla essence

1½ oz white chocolate (over 25% cocoa butter), grated

1½ oz milk chocolate (over 32% cocoa solids), grated

1½ oz dark chocolate (60–70% cocoa solids), grated

12 ovenproof espresso cups

SERVES 4

Preheat the oven to 300°F.

Put the milk, cream, and sugar in a medium pan and scald by bringing to just below boiling point. Remove the pan from the heat.

Beat together the egg yolks with the whole eggs in a large bowl, then beat in the scalded milk. Stir in the vanilla essence. Strain the mixture through a fine strainer and divide into 3 equal parts.

Flavor one-third of the custard with the white chocolate, one-third with the milk chocolate, and one-third with the dark chocolate, and stir each until the chocolate has dissolved. Divide each flavored custard between 4 of the espresso cups. Stand the cups in a roasting pan half-filled with hot water. Cover each cup with a small sheet of aluminum foil, or spread a large sheet over the whole roasting pan, tucking it in at the edges.

Bake for 20 minutes. The desserts are cooked with they are set around the edges but still slightly wobbly in the middle. If they're still not quite cooked, you may need up to 35–40 minutes, depending on your cups. Remove the foil, being careful not to let any condensed water drop onto the custards. Lift out of the roasting pan and let cool. Refrigerate overnight and bring to cool room temperature before serving.

For all those who love mint and dark chocolate, this is for you, especially if you're a fan of after-dinner mints covered in dark chocolate. The mousse is deceptively simple to make and is a good dinner-party standby. My niece adores this dessert—another winner for older children.

MINT CHOCOLATE MOUSSE

5 oz dark chocolate (60–70% cocoa solids)

4–6 dark chocolate-covered dinner mints (preferably After Eights), chopped

4 eggs, separated

2 tablespoons sugar

4 tablespoons heavy cream

1 teaspoon powdered gelatin

2 tablespoons chopped chocolate mint sticks, or frosted mint leaves and 1 cup heavy cream, to decorate

4 little pots or glasses

SERVES 4

Melt the chocolate with the dinner mints according to the instructions on page 17. Let cool slightly. Using an electric mixer, beat together the egg yolks and sugar in a large bowl until thick and mousselike, then beat in the melted chocolate-mint mixture and the cream.

Sprinkle the gelatin over 4 tablespoons water in a small, heatproof bowl and let soak and swell for 2–3 minutes. Put the bowl in a pan of simmering water and stir until the gelatin has dissolved. Beat into the chocolate-mint mixture.

Working quickly, beat the egg whites in a clean, dry bowl until stiff but not dry, then fold into the chocolate mixture with a metal spoon.

Divide the mousse between the pots. Scatter with the chopped mint sticks, then refrigerate until set. Alternatively, whip the 1 cup cream and use to decorate the mousses, along with the frosted mint leaves. Leave at cool room temperature for about 20 minutes before serving.

This is a great dessert to make when you've got some cranberries stashed in the freezer or during the Christmas season when they are fresh. Their fruity sharpness beautifully complements the chocolate. The result is a tempting, deep red compote hidden under a layer of darkest chocolate mousse. This is for adults only!

DRACULA'S DELIGHT

CRANBERRY COMPOTE

1 cup fresh or frozen cranberries

6 tablespoons sugar

2 tablespoons Cointreau

CHOCOLATE MOUSSE

6½ oz premium dark chocolate (60–70% cocoa solids)

3 tablespoons strong espresso

3 tablespoons unsalted butter, cubed

1½ tablespoons chocolate liqueur

3 large eggs, separated

four deep glasses or pots

SERVES 4

To make the cranberry compote, put the cranberries in a small pan with a splash of water and the sugar. Bring to a boil and simmer for 5 minutes until all the cranberries have burst and the compote is thick. Stir in the Cointreau, then spoon into the glasses. Let cool.

To make the chocolate mousse, melt the chocolate with the espresso and butter according to the instructions on page 17. Stir in the liqueur. Stir in the egg yolks while the chocolate mixture is still hot—this will cook them slightly.

Using an electric mixer, beat the egg whites in a clean, dry bowl until they form firm peaks. Using a metal spoon, stir a large spoonful of egg whites into the chocolate mixture to loosen it, then gently and evenly fold in the rest. Spoon the mousse on top of the cranberry compote. Cover and refrigerate for at least 6 hours or overnight.

This is chocolate divinity! Very rich and very smooth—use your favorite dark chocolate and you won't be disappointed. Make this for a special occasion, as it looks very elegant and can be made well ahead of time (although there is a lot of washing up to do). You can use white or dark chocolate for dipping the ladyfingers. Once this is set, I sometimes spoon a little chocolate liqueur over the ladyfingers before turning it out. You can even sprinkle the surface of the marquise with chocolate shavings. This makes a good birthday cake.

CHOCOLATE MARQUISE

8 oz dark chocolate (60–70% cocoa solids), plus 3½ oz for dipping

about 18 ladyfingers

6½ tablespoons unsalted butter, softened

½ cup sugar

2 tablespoons unsweetened cocoa

1 teaspoon good-quality instant coffee granules, ground to a powder

3 egg yolks

2 tablespoons chocolate liqueur, rum, or brandy

1¼ cups heavy or whipping cream

half-and-half, to serve (optional)

a 1-quart charlotte mold, soufflé dish, or 9 x 5 x 3-inch loaf pan, lined with nonstick parchment paper

SERVES 8

Melt the 8 oz chocolate and the 3½ oz chocolate separately according to the instructions on page 17. Let cool slightly until warm but not cold.

Dip the ends of the ladyfingers into the smaller amount of melted chocolate, tap off the excess and lay on a tray lined with waxed paper to set.

Line the sides of the prepared mold with the dipped ladyfingers, making sure they go in dipped tips first. You may have to shave down the last ladyfinger to give a tight fit.

Now have three mixing bowls at the ready. In one bowl, cream the butter with half the sugar until very white and fluffy. Beat in the cocoa and coffee powder.

In the second bowl, beat the egg yolks with the liqueur and the remaining sugar until really pale and doubled in volume.

In the third bowl, beat the cream until it forms soft peaks.

Beat the larger amount of melted chocolate into the butter mixture. Take a spoonful of the egg yolk mixture and beat it into the chocolate mix to loosen it, then fold in the remaining egg mixture. Finally, carefully fold in the cream. Pour the mixture into the mold. Tap gently to settle the mixture and refrigerate for at least 4 hours. Trim off any protruding ladyfingers, then turn out onto a plate to serve. It is rich enough on its own—but you could also serve it with half-and-half if you like.

There's something very special and exotic about the subtle marriage of chocolate and cardamom. Grinding the sugar, cocoa, and cardamom seeds together to a powder makes a perfumed and sophisticated coating for the surface. Grinding your own will give more flavor, but you can mix ready-ground cardamom with confectioners' sugar and cocoa for a similar effect. This is really one gigantic truffle, so it is best served cut into very thin slices.

CHOCOLATE CARDAMOM TRUFFLE CAKE

AMARETTI BASE

5 oz amaretti

½ stick (4 tablespoons) unsalted butter

5 tablespoons sugar

CARDAMOM TRUFFLE FILLING

2⅓ cups heavy cream

4–6 green cardamom pods, lightly bruised to open them

25 oz dark chocolate (60–70% cocoa solids), grated

½ stick (4 tablespoons) unsalted butter, cubed

4 tablespoons chocolate liqueur

CARDAMOM COCOA SUGAR

3 green cardamom pods

¼ cup sugar

⅓ cup unsweetened cocoa

a 10-inch cake pan with a removable base, base and sides lined with nonstick parchment paper

SERVES 10–12

To make the amaretti base, finely crush the amaretti in a food processor or put them in a plastic bag and crush with a rolling pin. Melt the butter and sugar in a pan over gentle heat, then stir in the amaretti crumbs. Press the mixture evenly over the base of the prepared cake pan and refrigerate for 20 minutes.

To make the cardamom truffle filling, put the cream and cardamom pods in a pan and heat until almost boiling. Remove from the heat and set aside to infuse for 20 minutes.

Meanwhile, put the chocolate and butter in a saucepan. Strain the infused cream through a fine strainer onto the chocolate (the cream will be warm enough to melt the chocolate). If it doesn't melt, warm over very low heat, stirring occasionally, but do not allow it to boil. Stir in the liqueur, then set aside until almost cold, but not set. With an electric mixer, beat the chocolate mixture for a couple of minutes—this will give a lovely airy texture. Pour onto the amaretti base. Let cool, then cover and refrigerate for at least 6 hours, or up to 48 hours before serving.

To make the cardamom cocoa sugar, remove the black seeds from the papery cardamom pods and put the seeds in a spice grinder with the sugar and cocoa. Grind to a powder. Carefully remove the cake from the pan and peel off the lining paper. Set on a chilled serving plate and sift the cardamom cocoa sugar evenly over the top. Serve immediately, cut into very thin slices.

This is another dessert that would make a wonderfully indulgent birthday cake adorned with golden candles. Children would probably prefer it made with really good-quality milk chocolate or you could stir white chocolate chips into the plain chocolate batter. It may seem against all chocolate rules to melt chocolate and water together (see page 17), but it works if they go in at the same time—the water keeps the chocolate fluid.

MARBLED CHOCOLATE CHEESECAKE

CHOCOLATE CRUMB CRUST

6 oz chocolate-coated graham crackers or chocolate chip cookies

5 tablespoons unsalted butter

2 tablespoons light brown sugar

MARBLED CHOCOLATE FILLING

5 oz dark chocolate (60–70% cocoa solids), chopped

25 oz full-fat cream cheese, at room temperature

1¼ cups sugar

1 vanilla bean, split lengthwise, seeds scraped out and set aside, or 1 teaspoon pure vanilla essence

2 large eggs

⅔ cup whipping cream and 3½ oz white chocolate, grated and chilled, to decorate (optional)

a 9-inch springform cake pan, lined with nonstick parchment paper

SERVES 10

Preheat the oven to 350°F. Carefully grease the sides of the springform pan and refrigerate until required.

To make the chocolate crumb crust, crush the graham crackers in a food processor or put them in a plastic bag and crush finely with a rolling pin.

Melt the butter and sugar in a small pan over gentle heat, then stir in the cracker crumbs. Press the mixture evenly over the base of the prepared pan. Bake for 15 minutes, then remove from the oven, lightly press the crumb crust down again, and let cool completely. Reduce the oven temperature to 325°F.

To make the marbled chocolate filling, melt the dark chocolate and 3 tablespoons water according to the instructions on page 17, then keep it warm.

Put the cream cheese, sugar, and vanilla seeds, if using, in a large bowl. Using a wooden spoon or electric mixer, beat until soft and creamy. Put the eggs and vanilla essence, if using, in a separate bowl and beat well. Gradually beat the eggs into the cheese mixture. Pour approximately 1 cup of the mixture into a small pitcher, then pour the remaining mixture into the springform pan.

Stir the warm chocolate into the reserved cheese mixture. Pour the chocolate mixture in a wide zigzag pattern over the surface of the cheesecake, edge to edge. Draw the handle of a thick wooden spoon through the pattern, zig-zagging in the opposite direction so the mixtures give a marbled effect. Do not overwork or the pattern will be lost. Keep it simple and the edges neat.

Bake for 20–25 minutes, or until the cheesecake starts to puff slightly around the edges but is still very soft in the center. Carefully transfer the tin to a wire rack and loosen the edges of the cheesecake with a thin-bladed knife. Let cool slowly by putting a large upturned bowl over the cheesecake. When completely cold, refrigerate for at least 3 hours before removing from the pan.

When you are ready to serve the cheesecake, remove it from the pan. For a special flourish, whip the cream and spread the sides lightly with a very thin layer. Press the grated white chocolate into the cream. Cut generous slices with a hot knife.

TRUFFLES AND CANDY

ITALIAN CHOCOLATE TRUFFLES

Look at the picture opposite and you will understand why a chocolate truffle is called a truffle—because it looks very like its dark and earthy savory sibling, the black truffle, and is just as precious to chocoholics. This is a classic truffle recipe—very rich and dense, and reliant on the best-quality chocolate that you can afford. For real truffle addicts, stir a little truffle honey or a drop of real truffle oil into the mixture—the flavor combination is quite mysterious but delicious—but keep them away from other chocolates as the flavor can wander!

5 oz dark chocolate (60–70% cocoa solids)

6 tablespoons salted butter, cubed

1 egg yolk

2 tablespoons Mozart Black Chocolate Liqueur or dark Crème de Cacao

1 teaspoon truffle honey or a drop of real truffle oil (optional)

unsweetened cocoa, to dust

a baking sheet, lined with nonstick parchment paper

MAKES ABOUT 15 TRUFFLES

Melt the chocolate according to the instructions on page 17. Beat in the butter, then the egg yolk, liqueur, and truffle honey, if using. Cover with plastic wrap and refrigerate for about 1 hour, or until set.

Sift some cocoa onto a plate. Using a teaspoon, scoop the chilled chocolate mixture into rough mounds, shape into a knobbly truffle shape in your hands, then drop into the cocoa. Roll it around until it is completely covered and put on the prepared baking sheet. Layer in an airtight container between sheets of nonstick parchment paper and refrigerate for up to 5 days or freeze for up to 1 month.

WHITE CHOCOLATE COCONUT TRUFFLES

These are delicious morsels of white chocolate married with coconut that has been infused with coconut liqueur. Look for Tropics Best organic coconut flour and shredded coconut: both are softer and nicer to eat than ordinary dried coconut. The truffles look best rolled in a shaggy coat of shredded coconut, but use more desiccated if you can't find it.

⅔ cup coconut flour (see above)

1 tablespoon clear Crème de Cacao (optional)

2–3 tablespoons coconut liqueur or white rum

½ teaspoon pure vanilla essence

½ stick (4 tablespoons) unsalted butter

3 tablespoons heavy cream

7½ oz white chocolate (over 25% cocoa butter), chopped

1 egg yolk, at room temperature

1 cup shredded coconut, to coat

a baking sheet, lined with nonstick parchment paper

MAKES ABOUT 20 TRUFFLES

Put the coconut flour in a bowl and pour over the liqueurs and vanilla essence. Mix well, cover, and set aside until the liquids have been absorbed.

Put the butter and heavy cream in a large, heatproof bowl over a pan of barely simmering water. The bowl should not touch the water. When melted, remove the pan from the heat and add the chocolate to the bowl. Stir until melted and smooth. Lift the bowl off the pan and stir in the egg yolk and the liqueur-infused coconut flour. Beat well, then let cool. When cold, cover with plastic wrap and refrigerate for about 2 hours until firm.

Spread the shredded coconut on a plate. Scoop up the white chocolate mixture and roll into 1-inch balls. Roll each truffle around in the shredded coconut to coat, then put on the prepared baking sheet, cover, and refrigerate for 1 hour. Layer in an airtight container between sheets of nonstick parchment paper and refrigerate for up to 5 days or freeze for up to 1 month.

I like to pass around a mound of these surprisingly warm and mysterious truffles instead of dessert. You could use pepper-infused vodka instead of the liqueur or brandy. Make your own chile vodka by infusing a couple of whole fresh whole hot red chiles, pierced here and there with a needle, in 1¼ cups vodka. Seal, leave in a cool, dark place for 2 weeks, then strain. The candied chile threads used to decorate these truffles are always a talking point. Remember that they can be very hot!

CHOCOLATE CHILE TRUFFLES

CHOCOLATE CHILE TRUFFLES

9 oz dark chocolate (60–70% cocoa solids)

3 tablespoons unsalted butter, cubed

1¼ cups heavy cream

1¾ teaspoons pasilla chile powder (see page 143)

2 tablespoons chocolate liqueur, brandy, or Armagnac

2 tablespoons unsweetened cocoa mixed with ½ teaspoon pasilla chile powder (see page 143) and 1 tablespoon confectioners' sugar, to dust

CANDIED CHILE THREADS

1¼ cups sugar

3 large, fresh red chiles, seeded and shredded

a baking sheet, lined with nonstick parchment paper

MAKES ABOUT 20 TRUFFLES

To make the chocolate chile truffles, melt the chocolate with the butter, cream, and chile powder according to the instructions on page 17. The mixture should be just tepid. Stir only occasionally (overmixing will make it grainy). Stir in the liqueur. Let cool until the mixture has thickened slightly, then beat for 2–3 minutes with an electric mixer. Refrigerate until firm.

Scoop out teaspoonfuls of the mixture and roll into balls. Put the truffles on the prepared baking sheet and refrigerate. Sift the cocoa-chile-sugar mixture onto a plate. Carefully roll each truffle in the powder, then set on a tray lined with nonstick parchment paper. Refrigerate until firm. Layer in an airtight container between sheets of nonstick parchment paper and refrigerate for up to 2 weeks or freeze for up to 1 month. Let stand at room temperature for 5 minutes before serving. Serve scattered with candied chile threads.

To make the candied chile threads, put the sugar and 1¼ cups water in a medium pan. Bring to a boil for 1 minute. Add the chiles to the sugar syrup, reduce the heat, and simmer for 25 minutes. Remove the pan from the heat and leave to soak in the syrup for 24 hours, if possible. Lift the chile threads out of the syrup with a fork, drain well, and arrange on nonstick parchment paper. Store in layers in an airtight container for up to 1 month.

COLETTES

I have tried in vain to find out the origin of the name of these pretty little truffles. All I know is that the French writer Colette was very fond of chocolate and real black truffles, so maybe these were named after her. I like to paint the cases with a layer of dark chocolate then a layer of white chocolate. They are fun to make and certainly have the wow-factor of a handmade chocolate. Use your favorite truffle mixture for the center if you prefer, or the recipe for Chocolate Ganache (page 136).

6½ oz dark chocolate (60–70% cocoa solids)
3 oz white chocolate
⅔ cup heavy cream
2 tablespoons chocolate liqueur, kirsch, brandy, or rum
20 amarena cherries, drained (optional)

a paintbrush
20 paper petits fours *cases or a chocolate mold with 20 indentations*
a piping bag fitted with a star tip

MAKES 20 COLETTES

Melt 3 oz of the dark chocolate and all the white chocolate, separately, according to the instructions on page 17. Using a paintbrush, paint the inside of the paper cases or chocolate molds thinly with the dark chocolate and refrigerate until set. Paint a coat of white chocolate on top of the dark and refrigerate until set.

Put the cream in a small pan and bring to just boiling point, then remove from the heat and add the remaining dark chocolate. Let the chocolate melt, then stir until smooth. Let cool, then stir in the liqueur. Let cool at room temperature for at least half an hour, or until thick enough to pipe. You can refrigerate the mixture briefly if you are short on time.

Put a cherry, if using, in each case. Beat the chocolate cream well, then spoon into the piping bag and pipe on top of the cherries. Refrigerate until ready to serve.

Carefully peel off the paper cases or pry the chocolates out of their molds to serve. Refrigerate in an airtight container for no more than 3 days.

CHOCOLATE COINS

These little treats are known in France as mendiants. *Each chocolatier has his or her own house specialty, so the sky's the limit when it comes to choosing the toppings. Make them as colorful as possible and don't forget to soak the dried fruits in lovely liqueur first.*

8 oz dark chocolate
ground chile and gold leaf, to decorate

SUGGESTED TOPPINGS
raisins, soaked in 1 tablespoon rum and ⅓ cup boiling water
crystallized ginger, chopped
slivered and toasted almonds
toasted hazelnuts and pistachios
salt crystals

MAKES ABOUT 20 COINS

Melt the chocolate according to the instructions on page 17. Remove from the heat and let cool for 3–4 minutes, or until very slightly thickened. Cover a large, heavy baking sheet with 2 layers of plastic wrap. Spoon 20 small pools of chocolate onto the plastic wrap. Let set for no more than 2 minutes, then scatter with toppings. Finish with a hint of ground chile and a touch of gold leaf. When the coins are completely set, ease off the plastic wrap. Serve with after-dinner drinks and coffee.

These are little mouthfuls of chewy caramel studded with fruit and nuts and dipped in your favorite type of chocolate. Mix and match the fruit and nuts, but make sure that some of the nuts are finely chopped to bind it all together. Florentines are a little tricky to make at first—you need to adjust your cooking times to suit your oven—but this becomes easy after the first batch. Once you serve them, they disappear in no time!

CHOCOLATE-DIPPED MINI FLORENTINES

8 oz mixed blanched almonds, hazelnuts, and pistachios

3 tablespoons unsalted butter

¾ cup plus 2 tablespoons granulated sugar

2½ tablespoons all-purpose flour

1¼ cups heavy cream

1 cup dried apricots, chopped, or candied mixed peel

⅓ cup dried sour cherries, dried cranberries, or quartered glacé cherries

8 oz dark chocolate (60–70% cocoa solids) or about 2½ oz each of white, milk, and dark chocolate

two 12-cup mini-muffin pans, greased and dusted with flour

MAKES ABOUT 100 MINI FLORENTINES

Preheat the oven to 375°F.

Chop half the nuts roughly and the remainder quite finely. Set aside.

Put the butter and sugar in a heavy-based pan and heat gently, stirring, until the sugar has almost dissolved (it will not dissolve completely). Add the flour and continue to stir over gentle heat until the mixture is smooth and comes away cleanly from the sides of the pan. Do not let the mixture catch or go brown. Remove the pan from the heat and slowly beat in the cream until smooth. Stir in the nuts, apricots, and cherries.

Drop half-teaspoonfuls of the mixture into the prepared mini-muffin cups. Be stingy with your measurements here—the florentines will spread. (You will need to bake the mixture in several batches.) Bake for 8–9 minutes, or until the florentines have spread and are bubbling and lightly brown at the edges. Remove from the oven. At this point the florentines will still be very soft. Let cool for a couple of minutes, then flip out of the pans with a small palette knife and let cool on a wire rack. Repeat with the remaining mixture.

Melt the chocolate according to the instructions on page 17. (If using different types of chocolate, melt them separately.) Dip the florentines halfway into the melted chocolate. Set them on a tray lined with nonstick parchment paper. Let set, then store them layered between nonstick parchment paper in an airtight container. Serve with after-dinner coffee and liqueurs.

This is a rich and decadent fudge for those with the sweetest of teeth to serve as a pick-me-up with midmorning coffee or after dinner with a chocolate liqueur. Nibble a chunk and let it melt on your tongue—heaven! If you don't have a sugar thermometer, boil the sugar mixture for 5–7 minutes to the "soft ball stage"—that is when a drop of mixture dropped into very cold water forms a soft ball that collapses when it is fished out of the water.

CHOCOLATE MAPLE FUDGE

2½ cups granulated sugar
6 tablespoons pure maple syrup
⅔ cup milk or cream
10 tablespoons unsalted butter, cubed
5 oz dark chocolate (60–70% cocoa solids), broken into pieces
2 teaspoons pure vanilla essence
salt crystals

a sugar thermometer (for best results)
a shallow 11 x 7-inch baking pan, lightly greased

MAKES ABOUT 2 LB

Have a large bowl of cold water ready in the sink.

Put the sugar, maple syrup, milk, butter, and chocolate in a large, heavy-based pan and stir over gentle heat, without boiling, until the sugar has dissolved.

Bring the mixture to a boil and boil hard until you reach 240°F on a sugar thermometer, stirring every now and then to prevent it burning. As soon as you reach this temperature, remove the pan from the heat and dip the base in the bowl of cold water to stop the mixture cooking. Add the vanilla essence and beat well with a wooden spoon until the fudge becomes thick and creamy, with a grainy texture. Pour into the prepared baking pan, smooth the surface, and let cool for 5 minutes. Press some salt crystals all over the fudge.

When it is almost set, score squares in the surface of the fudge with the tip of a sharp knife. When completely cold, turn out and cut into squares.

Variation: For a nutty alternative, fold in ⅔ cup chopped walnuts or pecans immediately after beating the fudge.

CHOCOLATE ALMOND-STUFFED FIGS

I like to dip these alternately in white and dark chocolate, but it just depends on your favorite types of chocolate and your mood.

20 large dried figs
3½ oz high-quality marzipan
1 tablespoon chocolate liqueur
20 whole almonds or walnut halves
8–10 oz dark chocolate (60–70% cocoa solids)

a large baking sheet, lined with nonstick parchment paper

20 paper cases

MAKES 20 STUFFED FIGS

Slit the figs open down one side with a sharp knife. Knead the marzipan and liqueur together and divide into 20 even pieces. Wrap each nut with a piece of marzipan and use to stuff the cavities of the figs, squeezing them into shape—don't worry if the filling protrudes.

Melt the chocolate according to the instructions on page 17.

Push a fig onto the end of a skewer or dipping fork and dip into the melted chocolate until lightly covered. Set on the prepared baking sheet and refrigerate until set. Place in paper cases and store in an airtight container, layered between sheets of nonstick parchment paper, at cool room temperature.

CHOCOLATE ARMAGNAC PRUNES

There's something fabulous about biting into these chocolate-dipped sweetmeats—the chocolate coating snaps to reveal the soft, rich Armagnac-infused prune with its creamy nut center. I don't recommend keeping these in the fridge, as they tend to go "sweaty."

20 Agen prunes (or other large juicy variety), pitted
6 tablespoons Armagnac, heated
6 tablespoons boiling water
20 whole almonds or walnut halves
8–10 oz dark chocolate (60–70% cocoa solids), chopped

a large baking sheet, lined with nonstick parchment paper

20 paper cases

MAKES 20 CHOCOLATE ARMAGNAC PRUNES

Slit the prunes open down one side with a sharp knife. Put in a medium bowl with the Armagnac and boiling water, and toss to coat them with the liquid. Put a saucer on top of the prunes to push them under the alcohol, then let soak for 2 hours.

Drain the prunes and pat dry on paper towels. Stuff the cavities with an almond or walnut and squeeze to enclose.

Melt the chocolate according to the instructions on page 17.

Push a prune onto the end of a skewer or dipping fork and dip into the melted chocolate until lightly covered. Set on the prepared baking sheet and refrigerate until set. Place in paper cases and store in an airtight container, layered between sheets of nonstick parchment paper, at cool room temperature.

CHOCOLAT
CHOCOLAT
CHOCOLAT
CHOCOLAT
CHOCOLAT

DRINKS, SAUCES, AND GLAZES

This is an instant mood lifter—make this drink when you are feeling a bit dejected and you cannot fail to feel fabulous. Watch out—it is quite potent! If you are feeling utterly miserable, the only answer is to top it with whipped cream and sink into comfort oblivion.

HOT SPICED RUM CHOCOLATE

2½ cups milk

2½ oz dark chocolate (60–70% cocoa solids), chopped

2 whole star anise

finely grated peel of ½ unwaxed orange

1 tablespoon orange-blossom or acacia honey

2½ oz spiced rum

1½ oz Grand Marnier or other orange liqueur

cinnamon sticks, to garnish (optional)

a large glass, warmed

a stainless steel spoon

SERVES 2

Put the milk, chocolate, star anise, orange peel, and honey in a pan and heat gently, stirring, until the chocolate has melted.

Remove and discard the star anise. Add the rum and Grand Marnier and liquidize in a blender or with a handheld blender until completely smooth and frothy. Pour into a warmed glass with a stainless steel spoon sitting in it to absorb the heat and prevent the glass from cracking. Garnish with cinnamon sticks, if using. Drink immediately and feel fabulous!

This drink can also be served chilled in the summer. Use 1¾ cups milk and heat as before but let cool (keeping the star anise in to infuse the milk). Remove the star anise, stir in the liqueurs, and pour into a blender filled with a handful of ice cubes. Blend until smooth, then pour into a chilled glass, sip, and feel restored.

Churros are long, golden, fingerlike Spanish doughnuts, deep-fried and rolled in sugar while still hot. They are eaten for breakfast, dipped into fantastically thick hot chocolate. They are also known as chi-chis *in Southwest France.*

SPANISH HOT CHOCOLATE WITH CHURROS

CHURROS (MAKES ABOUT 12)

3 cups all-purpose flour

1¼ cups milk

2 large eggs, beaten

vegetable oil, for deep-frying

superfine sugar or confectioners' sugar, to dust

SPANISH HOT CHOCOLATE

1⅔ cups milk

¼ teaspoon allspice

4 oz dark chocolate (60–70% cocoa solids), grated

2 egg yolks

a piping bag fitted with a large, fluted tip

a deep-fat fryer (optional)

SERVES 2

To make the *churros*, sift the flour onto a sheet of waxed paper. Put the milk and 1¼ cups water in a medium pan and bring to a boil. Pour in the flour and beat vigorously with a wooden spoon, stirring until the mixture just begins to pull away from the sides of the pan (just like choux pastry). Remove the pan from the heat and let cool a little.

Add the eggs and beat until the paste is completely smooth and not too runny (you may not need all of the egg).

Spoon the mixture into a piping bag. Heat the oil in a deep-fat fryer or wok until a piece of dough sizzles as soon as it hits the oil. Pipe fingers of the mixture into the hot oil, snipping off 4-inch lengths with kitchen scissors. Fry the *churros* in batches of 4–6 until golden brown, then remove with a slotted spoon and drain on paper towels. Put some superfine sugar or confectioners' sugar on a plate and roll the *churros* in it to coat. Eat immediately, dipping them into the hot chocolate. Any leftover *churros* can be frozen and reheated in the oven.

To make the Spanish hot chocolate, put the milk and allspice in a small pan and bring to a boil. Add the chocolate and stir until melted, then beat in the egg yolks. Stir over gentle heat until slightly thickened. Now beat with a handheld blender or a cappuccino frother, until frothy. Pour into cups and drink while hot. (Some say this is better made the day before and reheated.)

CHEEKY MONKEY CHOCSHAKE

This is a truly wicked, thick, alcoholic milkshake guaranteed to cheer up the chocoholic. I like to drizzle in extra warm chocolate sauce just before drinking it—stir with a long spoon and drink through a straw. If you didn't feel like a cheeky monkey before, you will after drinking this!

Bitter Chocolate Sauce (page 135), warmed

1 medium, ripe banana

2 oz Crème de Bananes

1½ oz clear Crème de Cacao

2 scoops vanilla or chocolate ice cream

2 tablespoons chocolate syrup or chocolate sauce

a good handful of crushed ice

a tall glass

SERVES 1

Peel the banana and break it into pieces.

Blend the banana, liqueurs, ice cream, chocolate syrup, and crushed ice in a high-speed blender. Serve in a tall glass drizzled with warm Bitter Chocolate Sauce.

CHEEKY MONKEY CHOCSHAKE (NONALCOHOLIC)

This is one for the kids, or if you are off alcohol.

1 medium, ripe banana

½ cup milk or banana yogurt drink

2 tablespoons chocolate syrup, chocolate sauce, or chocolate-nut spread

2 scoops vanilla or chocolate ice cream

a good handful of crushed ice

a tall glass

SERVES 1

Peel the banana and break it into pieces.

Blend the banana, milk, chocolate syrup, ice cream, and crushed ice in a high-speed blender. Serve in a tall glass.

CHOCOTINI

A must for all chocoholics—I doubt 007 would approve, but it's definitely one for a Bond girl!

unsweetened cocoa, to dip

2 parts vodka

1 part dark Crème de Cacao or other chocolate liqueur

a martini glass, chilled

a cocktail shaker

SERVES 1

Put some cocoa on a plate, wet the rim of the martini glass, and dip it in the cocoa.

Fill the cocktail shaker with ice and pour over the vodka. Put on the top and shake really well for 1 minute. Remove the top and strain into the glass. Now slowly pour the Crème de Cacao into the glass, being careful not to touch the rim. The chocolate liqueur will sink to the bottom making a two-tone layered cocktail. Serve immediately and sip slowly.

LE CHOCOLATIER

A cool chocolate hit for a hot summer night. Float some more chocolate liqueur on top if you are feeling really devilish.

1 part Mozart Black Chocolate Liqueur or dark Crème de Cacao

1 part white rum

5 oz premium dark chocolate ice cream

1 tablespoon grated dark chocolate

a tall glass, chilled

SERVES 1

Put the chocolate liqueur, white rum, and ice cream in a blender. Process at low speed until evenly blended and pourable. Pour into the chilled glass and sprinkle with the grated chocolate. Serve immediately.

THREE WARM CHOCOLATE SAUCES

WHITE CHOCOLATE SAUCE

This is one for all those who love white chocolate—it is very rich and sweet, so a little will go a long way.

1 cup light or heavy cream

6 tablespoons milk

8 oz white chocolate (over 25% cocoa butter), chopped

MAKES ABOUT 2½ CUPS

Put the cream and milk in a small pan and bring to just below boiling point. Remove from the heat and let cool for 2–3 minutes. Add the white chocolate and stir until completely melted. Serve warm.

If reheating, do so over gentle heat. Do not allow to boil or the sauce can thicken and seize.

BITTER CHOCOLATE SAUCE

The flavor of this sauce will rely on the type of chocolate you use, so choose it carefully. You may like to add a little sugar to sweeten it.

8 oz dark chocolate (60–70% cocoa solids), grated

¾ cup heavy or whipping cream

3 tablespoons unsalted butter, cubed

MAKES ABOUT 2 CUPS

Put the chocolate and cream in a small pan. Heat very gently, stirring occasionally, until melted and very smooth. Do not allow to boil. Beat in the butter and serve warm.

RICH CHOCOLATE FUDGE SAUCE

The only way to make a true fudge sauce is to include brown sugar. This gives it that fudgy taste and texture. I use cocoa here, as the sauce is boiled and chocolate would be too delicate to handle the heat.

⅔ cup heavy cream

¾ cup light brown sugar

¼ cup granulated sugar

½ cup unsweetened cocoa, sifted

3 tablespoons unsalted butter, cubed

1 teaspoon pure vanilla essence

a pinch of salt

MAKES ABOUT 2 CUPS

Put the cream, brown sugar, granulated sugar, and cocoa in a medium pan. Gradually bring to a boil, stirring occasionally. Turn down the heat and simmer gently for 1 minute, stirring to help the sugars dissolve. Stir in the butter, vanilla essence, and salt. Serve warm.

CHOCOLATE GANACHE

This is a very versatile frosting—it can be used to cover and fill cakes, make light truffles, and be piped into shapes. Needless to say it is very rich, and needs to be beaten to thicken and aerate it. Use according to the specific recipe.

1¾ cups heavy cream

8 oz dark chocolate (60–70% cocoa solids), grated

MAKES ABOUT 2¾ CUPS (ENOUGH TO FILL AND COVER A 9-INCH CAKE)

Put the cream in a heavy-based pan and bring to just boiling point. Add the chocolate and stir, then let stand for about 15 minutes, or until the chocolate has completely melted. Stir until smooth, then cover the surface with plastic wrap to prevent a skin forming. Let cool completely, then refrigerate until needed.

When you are ready to serve, bring to room temperature again, beat it lightly to soften (do not overbeat), and use according to the specific recipe.

GLOSSY CHOCOLATE GLAZE

A very useful glaze for dipping small cakes and cookies into, as it will stay soft and shiny. When using to cover a cake, let the glaze cool until it is starting to thicken and becomes spreadable, then use about one-third of the glaze to smooth over the cake and act as a primer for the final coat. Once you have spread over a rough base coat that fills in all the nooks and crannies, gently warm the glaze back to the ideal temperature (see below) and pour the whole lot directly onto the center of the cake. Spread it to the edges of the cake with a metal spatula and let it trickle over the sides naturally—you should have a streak-free cake. A cake turntable is useful here.

8 oz dark chocolate (60–70% cocoa solids), grated

1½ sticks (12 tablespoons) unsalted butter, cubed

1 tablespoon corn syrup

MAKES ABOUT 1⅔ CUPS (ENOUGH TO GLAZE A 10-INCH CAKE)

Melt the chocolate with the butter and corn syrup according to the instructions on page 17. If using to glaze a cake at room temperature, make sure the glaze is at the ideal temperature of 90–92°F. If using on a chilled cake, the glaze should be at 88–90°F.

CHOCOLATE CREME PATISSIERE

Here's a wonderful thick custard to use as a filling for all sorts of cakes and pastries. Make a plain version by omitting the cocoa and using a total of ¼ cup flour, cornstarch, or potato starch.

2½ cups milk
2 egg yolks
⅓ cup sugar
3 tablespoons unsweetened cocoa
2 tablespoons all-purpose flour, cornstarch, or potato starch
½ teaspoon pure vanilla essence

MAKES ABOUT 2¾ CUPS

Put the milk in a small pan and heat until just about to boil. Remove the pan from the heat. In a heatproof bowl, beat the egg yolks with the sugar, then beat in the cocoa and flour. Beat in the hot milk. Return to the pan and heat gently, stirring until starting to thicken. Once it reaches a very slow boil, simmer for 2 minutes, then stir in the vanilla essence. Use immediately or pour into a bowl, cover the surface with plastic wrap, let cool, then refrigerate for up to 1 week.

CREME ANGLAISE

This is a classic thin egg custard that can be served warm or cold with most desserts instead of cream. It can be left plain, infused with spices like cinnamon or cardamom, or flavored with a favorite liqueur.

1 vanilla bean, split lengthwise
1¼ cups milk
1 tablespoon sugar
2 egg yolks
2 tablespoons brandy, Armagnac, or bourbon (optional)

SERVES 4–6

Put the vanilla bean, milk, and sugar in a small pan and heat gently. Bring almost to a boil, then set aside to infuse for 15 minutes. Remove the vanilla bean. (Rinse and dry the vanilla bean and store in a sugar jar to make vanilla sugar.)

Put the egg yolks in a bowl, beat well, then pour in the infused milk. Mix well and return to the pan. Stir with a wooden spoon over gentle heat until the custard coats the back of the spoon. Pour into a cold bowl and stir in the brandy, if using. Cover the surface with plastic wrap, let cool, then refrigerate until needed.

Variations:

Chocolate Crème Anglaise: Stir in 1–2 oz grated dark chocolate once the custard has thickened. Once melted, stir in some chocolate liqueur instead of brandy.

Coffee Bean Sauce: Infuse 1 tablespoon finely ground espresso coffee with the vanilla bean, milk, and sugar.

CHOCOLATE BUTTERCREAM

This makes the smoothest, most heart-stopping buttercream ever, for filling or covering cakes and cookies. Be sure to leave plenty in the bowl for licking! It will keep for up to a week in the fridge and can be frozen for up to 6 months. Bring to room temperature before re-beating or it will curdle.

6 egg yolks
1 cup sugar
4 sticks unsalted butter, softened
6½ oz dark chocolate (60–70% cocoa solids), melted (see page 17) and cooled
3 tablespoons chocolate liqueur (optional)

a sugar thermometer (optional)

MAKES ABOUT 3 CUPS (ENOUGH TO FILL AND COVER A 9-INCH CAKE)

Using an electric mixer, beat the egg yolks until pale and creamy.

Put the sugar and ½ cup water in a small pan and heat gently, stirring occasionally, until the sugar has dissolved. Bring to a boil and boil hard until it reaches 240°F, or the "soft ball stage" on a sugar thermometer (see page 121). Immediately remove from the heat and pour the hot syrup onto the egg yolks in a thin steady stream, beating continuously until the mixture is a pale, thick mousse. Cream the butter in a separate bowl then beat in the melted chocolate. Beat this into the egg yolk mixture, then beat in the liqueur, if using. Use at room temperature, when it will be easiest to spread.

Variations:

White Chocolate Buttercream: Substitute the same amount of white chocolate for the dark chocolate and use a little vanilla or orange liqueur instead of chocolate liqueur.

Raspberry Buttercream: Take 12 oz frozen raspberries and thaw them in a strainer placed over a bowl. Press them gently with the back of a spoon to squeeze out the juice. Put the juice in a small pan and boil it hard until it has reduced to 3 tablespoons.

Press the raspberries through the strainer and mix the strained purée with the reduced raspberry syrup and a teaspoon of freshly squeezed lemon juice. Sweeten with sifted confectioners' sugar to taste. Beat this into the buttercream instead of the chocolate or even WITH the white chocolate. Use a little natural pink food color if the color isn't as bright as you would like.

GLOBAL CHOCOLATE AND THE FUTURE

For 3,000 years, chocolate had been a bitter drink venerated by the elite. By the midtwentieth century, due to the advances in chocolate-refining technology, chocolate could be manufactured on a vast scale to be eaten, not drunk. Drinking chocolate all but disappeared, leaving cocoa—a drink available to all—and the ubiquitous chocolate bar. This new commodity spread throughout the world and was pioneered by familiar names such as Fry and Cadbury in the UK, Menier and Poulain in France, Lindt and Suchard in Switzerland, and later, Hershey in the USA. Today, consumers are asking for more than ever—they want high-quality, organic, Fair Trade chocolate and they're willing to pay for it.

There is a revolution happening throughout the food world. We have begun to ask questions about what we are eating, where it has come from, and how it was produced. We are beginning to ask for quality and starting to recognize it—and the same is happening with chocolate.

In the past, in an attempt to manufacture a uniform product suitable for the mass market, cheaper and inferior beans were used, often unfermented, then over-roasted and conched for a long time to give a neutral but consistent flavor and smooth texture. Now, in the twenty-first century, we crave more than sweet, bland, creamy chocolate bars. We are rediscovering the true meaning of good chocolate through a burgeoning selection of independent factories using antique techniques and artisan chocolatiers employing state-of-the-art equipment. In their hands, the art of true chocolate-making is being kept alive and ever refined. We are in an age that is ceaselessly in search of the new, the different, the indulgent, the covetable. The consumer is becoming more demanding, chocolate-making is big business, and the industry has become very competitive. Larger manufacturers are realizing that they have to compete with these smaller, luxury producers to stay ahead of the game, so they have begun to produce their own specialist chocolate bars alongside their everyday products.

IT'S ALL IN THE GENES

"The spirit of chocolate is bringing us back to the true path." So says Murray Langham, author and chocolate creator. Who would have thought that chocolate has become so important to world economy that in the UK there is The International Cocoa Germplasm Database (ICGD). It sounds rather sci-fi, but it is an information service based at the University of Reading. The project aims to collate information on the origins, characteristics, and availability of cacao germplasm and to make this available to researchers. This conjures up images of rows of test tubes and labs full of glowing light, but in reality the germplasm bank is really a huge botanic garden. Research is done into cacao genes to trace the origins of the first wild plants and use their natural survival tools to improve susceptibility to pests and diseases in modern plants (which can decimate an entire harvest).

The second part of the ICGD is The International Cocoa Quarantine Centre, which operates to ensure that this international exchange of germplasm can be satisfied without transferring pests and diseases from one cacao-growing region to another. There are currently 350 clones available for exchange and a further 100 undergoing quarantine. The University of Reading took over responsibility for cocoa quarantine from the Royal Botanic Gardens at Kew in 1985 and receives funding from all over the world, supplying material for international clone and hybrid trials. The current quarantine procedure involves a two-year visual observation period to check for latent viral infections, and research is under way to accelerate the quarantine process. This research enables growers to experiment with improved varieties. In fact, due to some very clever research into Criollo, some growers, encouraged by enlightened chocolate companies, have been able to graft pure Criollo onto hardy Trinitario rootstock. This will mean that the king of cacao—the rare and coveted Criollo—will be able to be grown in quantity once more so real chocolate fanatics will be able to taste and experience chocolate aromas that haven't existed in the last 100 years. Domori, an Italian chocolate manufacturer, started replanting true Criollos in 1997 using seeds from the geneplasma bank in Trinidad. CIRAD (a French agricultural research center) is helping to revive the native Cacao Nacional plant in Ecuador and the Criollo in Madagascar. Chocolate bars boasting a content of a certain variety of bean will in future have to be genetically certified. This is all quite incredible, really—who would think that this amount of research is going into the humble chocolate bar?

So the future looks to be set in single-derivation chocolate bars made from "heirloom" beans, treated with respect at every stage of manufacture. Small production methods coupled with careful attention to harvesting, fermenting, roasting, blending, and grinding all combine to make good chocolate. Even the humble Forastero handled in the right way can make good chocolate, as the Swiss-owned Callebaut company has shown. Specialist or gourmet chocolate accounts for only 2% of the total world trade, and although it will never rival the sales in the mass market, there is and will be a blossoming choice out there, enough to suit every mood and palate.

FAIR TRADE CHOCOLATE

Today, good chocolate is fashionable, but at a price. It is expensive, but small-time growers certainly don't reap the rewards and some of them have actually never tasted a chocolate bar.

This is where the Fair Trade mark comes in. The Fair Trade mark is an independent consumer label that aims to guarantee a better deal for disadvantaged producers in the developing world. Fair Trade standards are set by the international certification body FLO (Fair Trade Labelling Organizations International).

It is worth remembering that not all Fair Trade products are organic and not all organic products are Fair Trade. The two certification systems are independent of each other.

ORGANIC CHOCOLATE

Even where products are not certified Fair Trade, many organic chocolate manufacturers do make a deliberate point of buying their cacao ethically (which is a good selling point for them), and many of them publicize this information on their products or websites. For example, Montezuma's has a "Trading Fairly" policy that includes ensuring that ingredients come from sources where growers get a fair price. Indeed buying organic chocolate is better for the environment from many points of view, and also may be better for health. Cacao is one of the most heavily sprayed crops in the world. Pesticides in developing countries can include chemicals such as lindane, which is linked to serious health problems including blood disorders and breast cancer. Organic cacao trees are grown with minimum use of pesticides—only four pesticides are permitted under organic production. This organic production should be encouraged in the tropical cacao-growing regions as it will sustain and preserve the surrounding biodiversity.

Organic chocolate often contains more cocoa solids than nonorganic chocolate, and it is not permitted to add any hydrogenated fat, known to be harmful to health and widely used in mass-produced brands. The emulsifier lecithin is a permitted nonorganic ingredient. Organic milk chocolate is made using organic milk products where high standards of animal welfare are adopted, including the infrequent use of antibiotics. Organic milk is higher in levels of some beneficial nutrients, particularly short-chain omega-3 essential fatty acids, as well as vitamin E and the antioxidant beta-carotene. Organic agriculture preserves the quality of the soil itself, so that foods produced often taste better and contain more nutrients. Organic products must be certified by a recognized certification body, for example The Soil Association. These bodies are regulated under EU law, and "organic" is defined in EU law. There are many organic certification bodies throughout the world. When a UK-certified chocolate manufacturer uses cacao beans from another country, the UK certifier will contact the overseas certifier, and will obtain inspection reports and details of inputs and outputs, to ensure that the overseas standards conform to EU standards. This process is called establishing "equivalence" and is rigorously applied. Suppliers of organic cacao beans are carefully certified and checked.

If the future is to be bright for chocolate and chocolate-growers we must learn the difference between good-quality and bad-quality chocolates, create a demand for high cocoa solids, be curious about bean varieties and how they are treated after harvest, and what the factory methods are. Better chocolates aren't overpowered by additional and unnecessary flavors. Good, true chocolate speaks for itself as it slowly melts on the tongue releasing all the aromas so carefully captured on its journey from bean to bar.

WEBSITES AND MAIL ORDER

GENERAL INFORMATION ABOUT THE COCOA TRADE

www.worldcocoafoundation.org

www.icco.org
The International Cocoa Organization

MISCELLANEOUS CHOCOLATE INFORMATION

www.mexicolore.co.uk
Wonderful site dedicated to teaching all things Aztec and Mexican. Costume and prop hire. Demonstrations and workshops. Delightful.

www.chocolatetherapy.com
New Zealand-based website with online chocolate shop. Change your chocolate—change your life! Visit for very interesting chocolate philosophy, psychology, and blog.

CHOCOLATE ONLINE

www.seventypercent.com
THE site for the chocolate lover—chocolate shop, forum, blog, info, and events—make this your homepage!

www.divinechocolateusa.com
The first Fair Trade chocolate company part-owned by cacao farmers in Ghana. Their mission is to improve the livelihood of smallholder cocoa producers in West Africa by establishing their own dynamic branded proposition in the UK and US chocolate markets. They strive to "make a quality and affordable range of Fair Trade chocolate bars accessible to chocolate lovers everywhere."

www.chocosphere.com
Internet-only chocolate shop based in Oregon, stocking Belgian, French, Venezuelan, Swiss, German, Spanish, Italian, and American chocolate bars, truffles, baking products, or gifts and gift baskets.

www.worldwidechocolate.com
Online shop selling chocolate from all over the world with a fantastic cocoa selection, including Mexican hot chocolate. Look in the Specialty Foods for some surprises.

www.chocolatesource.com
Online shop for worldwide chocolate, cocoa, nougat, and much more. Sells chocolate in small or large quantities. Ships to the USA and Canada only.

www.chocolat.com
Comprehensive shop for USA and European chocolate bars and cocoa.

www.beryls.safeshopper.com
Incredibly comprehensive selection of chocolate supplies, including cocoa, cacao nibs, cocoa butter, imported chocolate, chocolate colorings, thermometers, shavers and rufflers, gold and silver leaf, dragées etc.

www.chocolatealchemy.com
Informative and passionate chocolate site. Fairtrade cacao beans from the Dominican Republic, Ecuador, Ghana, Madagascar, Panama, Papua New Guinea, and Venezuela. Also cacao nibs, chocolate-making equipment, tools, and much, much more.

www.ediblegold.com
Gold and silver leaf sheets, flakes, and sprinkles.

www.gourmetsleuth.com
All sorts of chocolate-associated goodies, from black stone metates*, wooden* molinillos*, chocolate, chiles and chile powders to Mayan/Mexican drinking chocolate sets. Based in California but will export outside the USA.*

www.americanspice.com
Dutched cocoa, pasilla chile powder, and so much more—just look at the cinnamon!

www.fogcitynews.com/chocolate
455 Market Street
San Francisco
CA 94105
Tel: (415) 543-7400
The only newsagent in the world specializing in chocolate bars rather than newspapers. One of the largest collections of imported chocolate in the USA. Knowledgeable staff with tasting notes on a computer database. Well worth a regular visit if you're a local!

CONVERSION CHARTS

Weights and measures have been rounded up or down slightly to make measuring easier.

1 stick butter = 8 tablespoons = 125 g

Volume equivalents:

American	*Metric*	*Imperial*
1 teaspoon	5 ml	
1 tablespoon	15 ml	
¼ cup	60 ml	2 fl oz
⅓ cup	75 ml	2½ fl oz
½ cup	125 ml	4 fl oz
⅔ cup	150 ml	5 fl oz (¼ pint)
¾ cup	175 ml	6 fl oz
1 cup	250 ml	8 fl oz

Weight equivalents:

Imperial	*Metric*
1 oz	25 g
2 oz	50 g
3 oz	75 g
4 oz	125 g
5 oz	150 g
6 oz	175 g
7 oz	200 g
8 oz (½ lb)	250 g
9 oz	275 g
10 oz	300 g
11 oz	325 g
12 oz	375 g
13 oz	400 g
14 oz	425 g
15 oz	475 g
16 oz (1 lb)	500 g
2 lb	1 kg

Measurements:

Inches	*cm*
¼ inch	5 mm
½ inch	1 cm
¾ inch	1.5 cm
1 inch	2.5 cm
2 inches	5 cm
3 inches	7 cm
4 inches	10 cm
5 inches	12 cm
6 inches	15 cm
7 inches	18 cm
8 inches	20 cm
9 inches	23 cm
10 inches	25 cm
11 inches	28 cm
12 inches	30 cm

Oven temperatures:

110°C	(225°F)	Gas ¼
120°C	(250°F)	Gas ½
140°C	(275°F)	Gas 1
150°C	(300°F)	Gas 2
160°C	(325°F)	Gas 3
180°C	(350°F)	Gas 4
190°C	(375°F)	Gas 5
200°C	(400°F)	Gas 6
220°C	(425°F)	Gas 7
230°C	(450°F)	Gas 8
240°C	(475°F)	Gas 9